British economic performance 1945–1975

New Studies in Economic and Social History

Edited for the Economic History Society by
Michael Sanderson
University of East Anglia, Norwich

This series, specially commissioned by the Economic History Society, provides a guide to the current interpretations of the key themes of economic and social history in which advances have recently been made or in which there has been significant debate.

In recent times economic and social history has been one of the most flourishing areas of historical study. This has mirrored the increasing relevance of the economic and social sciences both in a student's choice of career and in forming a society at large more aware of the importance of these issues in their everyday lives. Moreover specialist interests in business, agricultural and welfare history, for example, have themselves burgeoned and there has been an increased interest in the economic development of the wider world. Stimulating as these scholarly developments have been for the specialist, the rapid advance of the subject and the quantity of new publications make it difficult for the reader to gain an overview of particular topics, let alone the whole field.

New Studies in Economic and Social History is intended for students and their teachers. It is designed to introduce them to fresh topics and to enable them to keep abreast of recent writing and debates. All the books in the series are written by a recognised authority in the subject, and the arguments and issues are set out in a critical but unpartisan fashion. The aim of the series is to survey the current state of scholarship, rather than to provide a set of prepackaged conclusions.

The series has been edited since its inception in 1968 by Professors M. W. Flinn, T. C. Smout and L. A. Clarkson, and is currently edited by Dr Michael Sanderson. From 1968 it was published by Macmillan as *Studies in Economic History*, and after 1974 as *Studies in Economic and Social History*. From 1995 *New Studies in Economic and Social History* is being published on behalf of the Economic History Society by Cambridge University Press. This new series includes some of the titles previously published by Macmillan as well as new titles, and reflects the ongoing development throughout the world of this rich seam of history.

For a full list of titles in print, please see the end of the book.

British economic performance 1945–1975

Prepared for the Economic History Society by

B. W. E. Alford
University of Bristol

Published by the Press Syndicate of the University of Cambridge
The Pitt Building, Trumpington Street, Cambridge CB2 1RP
40 West 20th Street, New York, NY 10011-4211, USA
10 Stamford Road, Oakleigh, Melbourne 3166, Australia

British Economic Performance 1945–1975 was first published by
The Macmillan Press Limited 1988
First Cambridge University Press edition 1995

Printed in Great Britain at the University Press, Cambridge

A catalogue record for this book is available from the British Library

Library of Congress cataloguing in publication data

Alford, B.W.E.
  British economic performance, 1945–1975/prepared for the
Economic History Society by B.W.E. Alford.
      p.   cm. – (New studies in economic and social history)
    Includes bibliographical references and index.
    ISBN 0 521 55263 X (hc). – ISBN 0 521 55790 9 (pb)
    1. Great Britain – Economic conditions – 1945–   I. Economic
History Society. II. Title. III. Series.
HC256.5.A735   1995
330.941′085–dc20   95–18849
                                                                CIP

ISBN 0 521 55263 X hardback
ISBN 0 521 55790 9 paperback

CE

Contents

Tables

Acknowledgements

I am grateful to William Ashworth, Rodney Lowe, Philip Richardson, L. S. Pressnell and John Wright for reading my manuscript and making many suggestions for its improvement. I have accepted most of their advice and the faults which remain are undoubtedly my own. Leslie Clarkson has been a model editor and Anne Griffiths an equally model secretary.

B.W.E.A.

Note on references

References in the text within brackets relate to the items listed in the Select Bibliography, followed, where necessary, by the page numbers in italics, for example (Keynes: *82*).

1
The overall picture

The performance of the British economy since 1945 has been the subject of an enormous amount of commentary and analysis. Much of it has been in the nature of self-examination: not least because the achievement of a high rate of economic growth became the central aim of political endeavour. Failure to match performance to expectations has developed into something of a national neurosis.

The literature throws into sharp relief the essential dichotomy in the approach to this issue between economics and economic history. Economic historians, in contrast to economists, are wholly concerned with the explanation of events in the real world over real time and in which irrationality and inconsistency, arising from imperfect knowledge or blind prejudice, are frequently dominant elements which cannot be assumed away by means of such abstractions as *ceteris paribus* (other things being equal) and rational time. These differences do not mean that economic historians are cast adrift in a sea of events: they possess the potentially powerful faculty of hindsight, though it can easily be a powerfully deluding one. For this reason the present analysis does not go beyond the mid 1970s. Not only does this give sufficient length of focus, it happens to match an important break in post-war economic experience, for Britain and for the world at large.

For almost the whole of the period under review, the prevalent and strongly held belief was that Britain, in common with other major economies, had climbed out of the economic slough of the interwar years and was set on a broad and permanent path of rising prosperity and full employment. Economic growth was both the watchword and the mechanism of this advance (Arndt, 1978; Kregel, 1972; Worswick and Ady, 1962). Economics provided the calculus for measuring it and the rules for its satisfactory regulation. These rules stated that the economic world was Keynesian – equally in the sense that Keynes had explained the fundamental laws of economic motion and that in the process he had provided the prescriptions which would render high unemployment and stagnation as things of the past (Posner, 1978). In the UK and the USA economists were transformed from being the apostles of the dismal science into the prophets of the new economic enlightenment.

Economic historians writing during this period did not escape these powerful influences. Past problems – in particular in the interwar depression – were analysed within a framework which might be termed a Keynesian hindsight model (Pollard, 1969; 1983). Post-war success, to the early 1970s, was credited to the skilful practice of Keynesian demand management (Maddison, 1964). Even the most circumspective analyst was optimistic in tone (Dow, 1964). But since the late 1970s these same events have come to be viewed somewhat differently (Morris, 1979; Wright, 1979). The devaluation of the dollar in 1971 and the oil crisis which came soon after it ushered in high unemployment and economic stagnation (Beckerman, 1979; Blackaby, 1979). For Keynesian economists confusion was further confounded when these were accompanied by galloping inflation. From 1955 to 1969 inflation averaged just under 2.8 per cent per annum. Between 1969 and 1973 the rate rose to 5.6 per cent, and to 24 per cent in 1975 (Graham, 1979). Ingenuity did not desert economists, however, and they diagnosed the new disease of stagflation (Meade, 1982).

It now seems more probable that until the beginning of the 1970s there was a combination of elements favourable to rapid economic growth in the major economies, particularly those of Europe and Japan. The main ones were post-war reconstruction, a productivity gap between the USA and the rest which drew American dollars and know-how into Europe and Japan, a sharp upward shift in peacetime levels of public expenditure (caused by defence needs and welfare transfer payments) and the absence of general synchronisation in the downswings which occurred in the major economies from time to time. Arising out of these conditions, and at the same time reinforcing them, was a widespread and buoyant expectation of continuous growth which was powerful enough to ride out random shocks (Allsop, 1979). Over the late 1960s, however, these elements began to weaken: the largely once-for-all gains from the first three had been absorbed whilst the fourth was ceasing to hold. Furthermore, the very economic success of Western European countries and Japan amounted to a major shift in the international balance of economic power in which the position of the USA was transformed from one of hegemony into one of *primus inter pares*. This was matched by increasing synchronisation in economic fluctuations such that the crises of 1971 and 1973 reverberated throughout the whole system with an effect stronger than anything experienced in peacetime for nearly half a century. Any assessment of Britain's economic performance has to take account of these powerful external forces.

In political terms economic growth involved the commitment to 'a high and stable' level of employment (Employment Policy, 1944). Performance itself soon established norms which by 1950 were higher than had been hoped for in 1945; and then, as European recovery got underway, the standard became even more precise and, for Britain, more formidable. Full employment gradually came to be thought of as a fact of life whilst percentage rates of growth of this or that economic measure became the punctuation of political rhetoric. Indeed, political argument, policy-making and economic analysis were suffused with an increasing flow of statistical data which in range and scale was quite unlike anything which had been experienced before: to such a degree that by the end of the period under review the rate at which data were being generated exceeded, probably by a wide margin, the capacity to apply them in practical economic action.

Historically the marked increase in the flow and quality of economic statistics was a valuable outcome of the war effort. The needs of war, however, were clear cut. Economic management was largely a matter of measuring resources of manpower and materials and adjudicating between bids made for them by the armed services and the major industries. How different have been the needs of peacetime (Robbins, 1947). An ever increasing flow of economic data has been matched only by the multifarious ways in which it can be interpreted and applied in relation to economic policy. Moreover, any extrapolation from data as a basis for policy runs the high risk that the demonstration of a relationship will sooner or later cause a modification of the actions which determine it. Thus policy based on statistical forecasts can easily be rendered counterproductive. But almost certainly the biggest problem is reliability. Close examination of even the main data series which form the canon of economic management soon reveals that they are subject to significant margins of error. In theoretical terms there are acutely difficult (and often insoluble) index number problems. In practical terms there is an age-old problem of accurate recording. Figures for the balance of payments, which have been at the heart of much policy discussion since the war, are an outstanding example of most of these difficulties (Dow, 1964; Cairncross, 1985).

With these reservations in mind, the following tables provide some broad measures of Britain's economic performance since 1945. They cover mainly the period since 1950 in order to allow for the full return to peacetime economic conditions which occurred largely during the reconstruction period after 1945. Nevertheless, it will be argued below that the nature and form of economic reconstruction had a powerful, long-term influence on British economic performance. Accordingly, detailed statistics for the years 1945 to 1950 are provided in Chapter 2. The basic measures of domestic economic performance are set out in Table I. The figures present something of a paradox. By previous standards they register a marked improvement and to this extent justify post-war hopes: in the interwar period GDP had grown at approximately 2 per cent p.a. (Matthews *et al.*, 1982) In comparative terms, however, they testify to a poor record, the cumulative effect of which was a decline in Britain's international economic status to a level undreamt of even as late as 1955 (Kravis, 1976; Stout, 1979).

Trade figures, despite the fact that they show a sustained increase in the volume of exports, tell a particularly sad story of relative decline for a once dominant trading nation (Table II).

The most controversial figures, yet the most crucial for the analysis of Britain's growth record, concern the elusive concept of productivity. The main aggregate measures are shown in Table III.

Table I *UK comparative economic performance 1950–73*

| | (i) Average % growth in GDP per annum | | | | |
	1950–5	1955–60	1960–4	1964–9	1969–73
UK	2.9	2.5	3.1	2.5	3.0
France	4.4	4.8	6.0	5.9	6.1
Germany	9.1	6.4	5.1	4.6	4.5
Italy	6.3	5.4	5.5	5.6	4.1
Japan	7.1	9.0	11.7	10.9	9.3[a]
USA	4.2	2.4	4.4	4.3	4.4

Sources: A. Cairncross, 'The Postwar Years 1945–77', in R. Floud and D. McCloskey, *The Economic History of Britain since 1700.* Vol. 2 (Cambridge, 1981), p. 376; (Jones, 1976, 80).
[a] GNP

| | (ii) National income per head 1960 and 1973 UK = 100 | | | | | |
	UK	France	Germany	Italy	Japan	USA
1960	100	92	91	51	34	206
1973	100	124	144	68	94	164

Source: Prest and Coppock, 1982, *197.*

Table II *UK comparative trade performance 1945–75*

| | (i) % shares of world exports of manufactures | | | | |
	1950	1960	1965	1970	1975
United Kingdom	25.5	16.5	13.9	10.8	9.3
France	9.9	9.6	8.8	8.7	10.2
Germany	7.3	19.3	19.1	19.8	20.3
Japan	3.4	6.9	9.4	11.7	13.6
USA	27.3	21.6	20.3	18.5	17.7

Source: (Blackaby, 1979, *241*)

(ii) Volume of UK exports 1963 = 100			
1945	20	1965	108
1950	75	1970	140
1955	80	1975	182
1960	90		

Source: Economic Trends.

Table III *Comparative productivity measures 1955–73 (Average % rates of growth per annum)*

			(i) GDP per person employed				
	UK	Austria	Belgium	France	Germany	Italy	Netherlands
1955–60	1.8	4.2	2.1	4.9	5.0	4.6	3.5
1960–4	2.2	4.6	4.1	5.0	4.7	6.3	3.4
1964–9	2.5	5.2	3.6	5.2	5.0	6.3	4.8
1969–73	2.8	6.4	4.2	5.0	4.2	4.5	4.4

(*Source:* Jones, 1976, p. 82)

	(ii) GDP per man year	
	USA	Japan
1951–64	2.5	7.6
1964–73	1.6	8.4

Source: (Matthews *et al.*, 1982, *31*).

The most exhaustive exercise of this kind centres on measuring productivity growth by methods developed by economists in the 1950s and 1960s (Denison, 1968; Matthews *et al.*, 1982). The sources of growth of gross domestic product (GDP) are divided into labour, capital and productivity. The difference (positive or negative) between the rate of growth of GDP and the combined, weighted rate of growth of inputs of labour and capital, known as total factor input (TFI), gives the rate of growth of productivity. The difference is defined as total factor productivity (TFP) because it is the change in output resulting from changes in the way in which quantities of capital and labour are employed and not from changes in the quantities themselves (Table IV).

As a broad measure of economic performance this analysis has some value. It exposes, for example, marked differences between the pre- and post-war periods in the UK. But the severe limitations of this technique become clear when account is taken of the conditions which would have to hold in order to render the results accurate. (Totally homogenous capital and labour markets; constant returns to scale over all ranges of output; marginal productivity pricing for all factors; continuous variable relationships between factors over time; land as an insignificant input.) Quite

Table IV UK growth of total factor productivity 1924–73 (Average % growth per annum)

(i) The economy as a whole

	Labour (man hours)	Capital		Total factor input		GDP	Total factor productivity	
		Gross	Net	Gross capital	Net capital		Gross capital	Net capital
1924–37	1.5	1.8	2.0	1.5	1.6	2.2	0.7	0.6
1937–51	0.1	1.1	1.3	0.4	0.5	1.8	1.4	1.3
1951–73	-0.5	3.2	3.9	0.5	0.7	2.8	2.3	2.1

(ii) Manufacturing industry

	Labour (man hours)	Capital (gross)	Total factor input[a]	Output	Total factor productivity
1937–51	1.0	2.9	1.6	2.5	0.9
1951–64	0.2	3.3	1.2	3.2	2.0
1964–73	-1.6	3.3	-0.1	3.0	3.1

Source: (Matthews et al., 1982, 208, 228–9).
[a] Weighted combination of labour and capital.

apart from these constraints there are more familiar problems associated with compound growth calculations: the weighting of capital and labour is on the crude basis of their respective shares in gross domestic income; the technique of weighting from year to year is, as always, a compromise between different types of index; compound rates of change are constant over a given period and, therefore, may not adequately reflect sharp movements within the period. In terms of historical explanation the last difficulty is particularly important since TFP analysis pulsates to the rhythm of the sub-period and, as subsequent discussion will show, this constitutes a major problem for the so-called war period of 1937–51.

While recognising these problems practitioners of TFP analysis still claim that TFI and TFP, taken together, can tell us useful things about economic performance. But precisely how are the results to be interpreted? What is presented, like much in economic analysis, is an identity (TFI + TFP = GDP) and not a causal relationship. Any one or pair of these elements can be causal, and these relationships may change within the period being measured. Realistically, the process is multiplicative and not additive and it is subject to a complexity of varying lags. More specifically, considerable ambiguity attaches to the meaning of the term total factor productivity. In early studies it was called the residual – as such, it had more direct meaning, being no more nor less than a bundle of factors which cannot be quantified individually. It includes advances in knowledge, personal characteristics such as effort and experience, union power, government regulations. What are these other than the very stuff of economic development? And the striking, though perhaps not surprising fact, is that the residual (TFP) is usually the largest term in the identity.

The remaining measure of economic performance is aggregate domestic investment. Since 1945, Britain's record has been consistently better than that which she achieved in the interwar years – an average of 20 per cent of GDP as compared with 11 per cent (Matthews *et al.*, 1982). Yet again, however, in international terms Britain's record is far less impressive – over the late 1960s and early 1970s the averages were Japan 39%, West Germany 28%, France 27%, Netherlands 27%, Belgium 25%, Italy 21%, USA 18% (Caves and Krause, 1980). Moreover, the low figure for the

USA has to be seen against a much higher level of *per capita* income. It is necessary to stress, however, two specific problems connected with these figures. First, the collection of data depends heavily on published financial accounts which are produced for the quite different purpose of minimising company taxation, with corresponding differences in the definition of capital. From a national accounting viewpoint the distortions arising from this are probably large. Secondly, there are enormous index number problems in constructing price series for capital goods.

In sum, Britain's economic record since 1945 represents a notable improvement on the interwar period, but increasingly it fell well short of current expectations and the achievements of our major competitors. How this shortfall is to be accounted for forms the focus of the survey and analysis which follow. Moreover, it is not just a matter of explaining comparative failure. The degree of failure has led to differences in absolute levels of economic performance between Britain and most of the advanced economies, which have begun to alter the relationship between them.

As has been indicated above, there is a vast array of literature on the topic of Britain's post-war economic performance. Our analysis will seek to show, however, that much of the literature is concerned either with providing different (often ingenious) ways of measuring the fairly obvious symptoms of economic malaise, or with reports on how the 'British disease' of low growth and low productivity has affected various parts of the economy. In medicine, measurement and observation often lead to diagnosis and cure, though not invariably so. Certainly the British economy still awaits a convincing diagnosis of its ills.

The various statistical measures of performance which have been produced have indirectly served to reveal the crucial and probably dominant role of non-quantifiable influences in economic performance. Hence, our analysis will cover such issues as social and cultural attitudes, social structure, the role of economic ideology, the nature of the educational system, and the nature and operation of business corporations, the senior civil service and trade unions. It will be shown, however, that clear understanding of how, precisely, these factors affect economic performance is extremely difficult. But before turning specifically to this task, we must examine a little more closely the events of the immediate post-war years.

2
Post-war crises and reconstruction

Britain, alone among the European nations, joined in the military victory of the USA over the Axis powers. But in economic terms the relationship was different. Britain, in common with Europe and Japan, faced the daunting task of promoting economic recovery. By contrast, in the act of saving Europe from itself, the USA stimulated its own economic recovery from the collapse of the 1930s to such a level that by 1945 its economic strength presented the major barrier to economic recovery for the industrialised world.

The war caused a massive distortion in the deployment of resources when compared with peacetime conditions. For obvious reasons the use of manpower was particularly affected. Accordingly, manpower budgeting became the central task of wartime planning. Table V shows the main changes which occurred as a result of this activity. The armed forces absorbed way above the equivalent of both the natural and stimulated increase in the labour force. As between civil occupations, there was a massive shift of workers into war-related jobs. Some industries lost heavily. Building and civil engineering experienced virtually a 50 per cent reduction, whilst even the clothing industry suffered the loss of over one-third of its pre-war workforce. These and the other changes presented enormous difficulties in the immediate post-war years. Manpower shortages were acute in agriculture, textiles and coal-mining – the last of which had not performed well during the war mainly, though not entirely, as a result of a shortage of miners and an ageing labour force.

Substantial readjustments had occurred by 1948, as Table V shows. Even so, the process operated under conditions of acute

Table V *Changes in manpower use 1938–48 (000s Great Britain)*

	1938	1944	% of 1938	1948	% of 1938
Armed forces and auxiliary services	385	4,967	1,290	846	219
Total in civil employment	17,378	16,967	98	19,064	110
Agriculture and fishing	949	1,048	110	1,123	118
Mining and quarrying	849	813	96	839	99
Metals, engineering, vehicles, shipbuilding	2,590	4,496	174	3,546	137
Chemicals, explosives, paints, oils, etc.	276	515	187	367	133
Textiles	861	635	74	835	97
Clothing, boots, shoes	717	455	63	613	85
Food, drink, tobacco	640	508	79	628	98
Cement, bricks, pottery, glass	271	159	59	263	97
Leather, wood, paper	844	536	64	775	92
Other manufacturers	164	129	79	223	136
Building, civil engineering	1,264	623	49	1,375	109
Gas, water, electricity	240	193	80	275	115
Transport and shipping	1,225	1,237	101	1,472	120
Distributive trades	2,882	1,927	67	2,354	81
Commerce, banking, insurance, finance	414	268	65	344	83
National and local government	1,386	2,091	151	2,229	161
Miscellaneous services	1,806	1,334	74	1,813	136
Registered insured unemployed	1,710	54	3	272	16
Total working population	19,473	22,008	113	20,367	105

Source: Annual Abstract of Statistics.

economic difficulty which, combined with a lack of understanding on the part of the government, stored up problems for the future. Thus while labour productivity in terms of gross domestic product per head grew at 1.5 per cent per annum between 1945 and 1951 (and by 2.5 per cent per annum between 1948 and 1951) it will be shown that these gains hardly nibbled at the chronic problems of overmanning in British industry (Chapters 3 and 5 below). Indeed, manpower shortages in the immediate post-war years were calculated almost wholly in terms of job vacancies based on existing techniques and work practices.

Capital shortage was a closely inter-related problem with labour supply. War losses, the physical rundown of assets and the reduced capacity of the economy to generate savings and investment, all played their part. For example, Britain lost just over one-third of her shipping tonnage; pre-war overseas income had paid for one-quarter of imports, whereas, during the war one-quarter of overseas assets had been disposed of and other substantial assets were put out of commission (such as plantations in the Far East). War debts (including substantial balances owed to sterling countries) amounted to £3,500m which was the equivalent of 40 per cent of gross national product in 1945 (Sayers, 1956). The net change in capital account was approximately £4,700m which, overall, made Britain an international debtor for the first time since the eighteenth century. To add to this agony, in August 1945 the USA withdrew Lend Lease, the scheme through which essential war supplies had been made available to Britain.

Little wonder that throughout the war and post-war period there was a persistent fear of inflation. Politicians and officials alike were haunted by the record of the First World War in which inflationary excess was seen to have brought its nemesis in subsequent deflation and massive unemployment. Price control and enforced saving (mainly through consumer rationing) thus became powerful instruments of wartime planning. Prices rose by one-and-a-half times during the course of the war, which represented a significant achievement by the authorities. The danger remained acute, however. After all during the First World War prices had been held to a twofold increase: the inflationary explosion had occurred immediately after the war. The potential for inflation after 1945 was great because the productive capacity of the country had been distorted and damaged.

These brief indications drawn from the literature leave no doubt as to the scale of the problems facing the Labour government elected in a landslide victory in 1945. These were not just domestic

Table VI *The pattern of economic recovery 1946–51: indices of output (1938 = 100)*

	1946	1947	1948	1949	1950	1951
Agriculture, forestry and fishing	111	116	114	123	126	128
Mining and quarrying	78	80	85	88	89	91
Manufacturing	105	111	121	128	137	143
Building and contracting	77	80	87	91	91	88
Gas, electricity and water	134	139	148	158	172	183
Distributive trades	82	88	92	98	162	100
Insurance, banking, finance	98	103	104	106	112	113
Professional and scientific services	102	106	111	116	122	125
Miscellaneous services	84	86	87	83	82	82
Public administration and defence	240	176	153	149	144	152
Gross domestic product	105	106	111	115	119	122

Source: (Feinstein, 1972).

problems but were part of Britain's larger task of achieving recovery in its international economic position (see Chapter 6). The economic record of the period 1945–50 which is summarised in Table VI bears testimony to the progress which was achieved in recovering from the depredations of the war. In judging this record there has been a strong tendency among commentators, from either an economic or a political viewpoint, to award the Labour government good marks for achievement (Morgan, 1984; Cairncross, 1985). As will be shown, however, it is an assessment open to serious question. And the matter certainly cannot be resolved until much work has been done, especially on individual firms and industries.

A major temptation is that of drawing up – either explicitly or implicitly – a balance sheet of war. Qualitative judgements are then derived from the positive or negative outcomes of the quantities involved. Hence, it has been pointed out that there was no net increase in total real wealth between 1913 and 1951, and in this context the world wars are cast as the harpies which devoured the accumulated efforts of previous generations. Yet such an assessment ignores the independent forces at work in the interwar years which caused economic performance to fall well below economic potential; it also fails to take into account the record of poor growth over at least a quarter-century before 1914. Quite apart from these omissions, the balance sheet appraisal ignores the economic impact of war on attitudes, expectations and the behaviour of institutions, which might well have operated in the opposite direction.

The uncertain nature of the economic impact of the Second World War is easily demonstrated. From the late 1940s to the early 1970s, the economies of Western Europe and Japan experienced unprecedented growth. All had suffered devastating effects from the war. If the war was not the cause of that subsequent economic growth – either wholly or in part – then clearly it did not seriously inhibit it. Moreover, it has already been argued (in Chapter 1) that there was a combination of influences at work internationally during those years which was conducive to rapid expansion, some of which arose directly from the war.

Despite the crises of the period 1945–50, these years can also be seen as ones of great opportunity. In comparison with the 1930s Britain was in an ascendent political position in Europe and she enjoyed considerable economic advantages over her main rivals. In 1948, for example, the UK accounted for 42 per cent of Western European exports. Put another way, UK exports were nine-and-a-half times the West German level. But from then on the position declined rapidly and by 1951 UK exports were only double the West German level (Milward, 1984). It is the combination of crisis and hard-won achievement on the one hand, and the probability of lost opportunities on the other, which calls for further comment.

Many writers have noted the widespread changes in ideas and attitudes that occurred between 1939 and 1945 (Addison, 1977). The Second World War, unlike the First, was a people's war waged against a hideous ideology. As such, it engendered both the commitment and the determination to create new peacetime conditions in which the political and economic failures of the 1930s would truly become things of the past. In Britain, this meant a commitment to increased social welfare, a high and stable level of employment, and more even distribution of income and wealth through a system of progressive taxation. The totems of this new world were the Beveridge Report (1942) and the White Paper on Employment Policy (1944) (Harris, 1977; 1981). All of which prompts the obvious question: how fundamental were these changes?

Many parts of the Beveridge Report were not new. It presented an extended and more clearly structured form of much which already existed. Most crucially, the report still viewed unemployment as something requiring periodic relief rather than with a sense of understanding of how relief and cure were bound up together. It made the rough and ready assumption that the underlying cure of unemployment would be provided by Keynesian economics. Nevertheless, for a number of writers the essential point is not so much that these ideas on unemployment and social welfare were new, as that a broad political consensus developed around them which achieved its apotheosis in the triumph of Keynesianism in 1947 (Booth, 1983; 1984). There is, however, accumulating evidence which suggests a somewhat different interpretation of events.

The Employment Policy White Paper was certainly a major declaration of intent but effective consensus also requires agreement over means. This was not achieved for a number of reasons. First, the intent was vague: 'high and stable' not full employment was the aim. Even for the optimists this allowed for unemployment rates of up to 8 per cent. Secondly, whilst a wide measure of agreement on policy had existed among economic officials during the war (especially within the Economic Section of the Cabinet Office), this was conditioned by the limited scope of wartime circumstances and did not extend to peacetime policies. In large part lack of consensus reflected differences in theoretical positions; to some degree it was a consequence of the different interests of the departments within which economists were employed. Thirdly, there has been a tendency in the literature to overestimate the practical influence of economists (Booth, 1983; 1984; Cairncross, 1985). This results from a kind of double vision which blurs the difference between the historical interpretation of contemporary economic advice and the evaluation of ideas which *subsequently* proved to be significant in the evolution of economic theory.

More importantly, recent research reveals a major lack of consensus among politicians over the basic role of government in the economy (Harris, 1981). Indeed, it was directly as a consequence of this that the White Paper was so general in approach and so nebulous on crucial issues. The broad difference was between those who advocated some form of centralised planning and those who wished to see the government as the final umpire of a largely free market. Intermixed with this division were differences which stemmed from strong commitments to domestic policies of social welfare on the one hand and the belief that Britain should pursue a world role on the other. Much of the rhetoric of the war effort had been imperialistic and the imperial idea retained strong political allegiance after 1945 especially on the right of British politics. Paradoxically, it received support, also, from the left for whom Commonwealth ties were an important part of their anti-Americanism (Gardner, 1969; Louis, 1977).

The Labour Party and the Labour government were explicitly committed to planning, but what planning meant was not precisely defined or theoretically established (Cairncross, 1985). The concept obviously implied certain practical requirements: regulated markets, allocation of materials, production targets, manpower planning – all of which would be operated through some structure of planning machinery. Furthermore, international forces bore so heavily on the economy that some kind of centrally planned response seemed unavoidable. It is clear, moreover, that Keynesian economics, with its focus on the internal management of short-term equilibrium, was not the theory to match such a political prescription.

For the government, acceptance of central planning did not stand or fall on the issue of nationalisation. In carrying through its programme it honoured certain political debts, especially to the miners (Morgan, 1984). But ideologically, nationalisation became something of an irrelevance since both major political parties accepted that some form of state control and assistance was essential for coal, rail transport, electricity, gas, civil aviation, cable and wireless, and the Bank of England. In all of them, nationalisation was the end of a process which had started well before the war (Ashworth, 1986; Hannah, 1982). In its implementation, beginning with the Bank of England in 1946, economic and commercial requirements were secondary to the aim of establishing workable administrative structures though this task alone was a formidable one (Chester, 1975). There is certainly no evidence of nationalisation being seen, or used in practice, by the government as a takeover of the commanding heights of the economy from which economic planning could be directed. Significantly, the one industry – iron and steel – for which nationalisation was a real ideological issue, proved to be only a temporary state acquisition. To some degree perhaps, the nationalisation of the Bank of England was regarded as a crucial step in gaining control of banking and finance. But, as will be seen later, the reverse would be nearer the truth.

In other areas, early peacetime policy had the trappings of a form of economic planning (Worswick and Ady, 1952). Everywhere there were shortages and, with the post-First World War period much in mind, there was a fear of inflation in the very short run, followed by deflation in the medium term. The war had required a high degree of economic planning, much of which was carried over into peacetime. First and foremost this involved a whole battery of controls over production and consumption. Secondly, under Dalton as Chancellor of the Exchequer, a policy of cheap money was adopted in 1945 to guard against medium-term deflation and to keep down the cost of borrowing. The policy relied on the government being able to meet its borrowing requirements through persuading the public to take up successive issues of government loan stock and through internal (or technically known as departmental) support. But with a sharp rise in the budget deficit and a strongly declining public appetite for loan stock, the government had to issue Treasury bills and Treasury deposit receipts on a scale which pushed liquidity to high levels. Controls over investment goods and capital issues held the ring but only until 1947; at that point interest rates had to be allowed to rise (Cairncross, 1985). Thirdly, the wartime invention of national income accounting provided the opportunity for producing more precise measures for forward planning. This was taken up by the Economic Section of the Cabinet (under Meade) which devised the *Economic Survey*: the expected level of output for the following year was predicted on the basis of the estimated changes over the present year in individual sectors of the economy. The first survey made its appearance in 1946 (Dow, 1964). Finally, an active regional policy was introduced through the agency of the Board of Trade. It was a continuation, in effect, of the 1930s Special Areas policy (which had received further impetus from the Barlow Report on industrial location) and from the carry-over of wartime controls which gave the government far more effective power in this sphere than it had ever possessed (Brown, 1972).

Would-be practitioners of planning did not clearly understand the constraints imposed on their activities by external economic relations and pressures. Britain had played a major part in the Bretton Woods agreement which, through the establishment of the International Monetary Fund, led to a major role for sterling as a reserve currency (Eckes, 1975); and in 1945, after considerable debate, it had opted for a large US loan ($3.75bn plus $650m in settlement of Lend-Lease obligations) as against tighter domestic restrictions on consumption, to help to overcome post-war shortages of goods and materials. It is perhaps a little too easily accepted by most commentators that because of the desire of the population at large to receive some immediate economic benefit from having won the war there was no alternative to seeking an American loan. But with or without an American loan the issue of the external constraint turns on Britain's obligations to the sterling area (Bell, 1956). Central to these were the sterling balances which were liabilities which had accrued during the war largely to poorer countries within the Commonwealth. Although Keynes at one stage suggested that some part of the sterling balances should be cancelled, the idea was never taken up. Likewise no scheme for seeking American assistance in getting rid of sterling balances was made a serious part of the loan negotiations, even though there are many indications of US suspicion of the sterling area and willingness to assist in its dismantlement (Van Dormael, 1978). Keynes and his associates in Washington – in accordance with government views at home – fobbed off American suggestions with vague promises for the future. Whatever their regrets at the time, however, the Americans had certainly lost them by the early 1950s as they came increasingly to value the sterling area as a buffer for the dollar. Whilst Britain was genuinely concerned about honouring its debts there was a high mindedness about it which shut out any consideration of alternatives which, by reducing the obligation to maintain the value of sterling, would have given more scope for domestic planning.

Contemporary perception was influenced by immediate demands and needs and these served indirectly to reinforce the determination to play a leading role in the world – a determination based on desire rather than understanding. Britain, in common with the Allies, had learned from the First World War that international peace and stability could only be maintained by the early restoration of Germany to the comity of nations. At the same time Britain, with the USA, had stood against Europe and was understandably unwilling to enter directly into close political union with it. Ernest Bevin, the new Foreign Secretary, was particularly suspicious of any form of European political integration which he thought would be easy prey for continental communist parties (Bullock, 1983). The cornerstone of his policy was the Atlantic Alliance and this required large armed forces to enable Britain to fulfil its chosen world role. Sterling, as tradition dictated, became an essential element in this form of the *Pax Brittanica*. If this was delusion it was given a sense of realism in the immediate post-war world through the UK economy being clearly stronger than the economies of either Europe or Japan (Barnett, 1972; Maddison, 1984).

In 1947 the problems of persistent shortages turned into a crisis. In particular, coal stocks had sunk to a level below that at which distribution and use could operate efficiently. The shortfall was mainly a consequence of low output over the last two years of the war; and the harsh winter of 1946/7 was the last straw. The industry simply could not produce enough coal to meet the economy's needs (Ashworth, 1986). Crisis became potential disaster with the approach of the date from which controls on the free exchange of sterling for dollars would be removed (convertibility). This placed an increasing pressure on the exchange rate causing a loss of reserves and the exhaustion of the American loan which burst into a massive drain once convertibility came into operation in July. Britain's rescue drew it deeper into the American orbit, though with the introduction of Marshall Aid to promote the economic recovery of Europe by means of financing balance of payments deficits, this was to a degree common to western European countries (Milward, 1984). Inevitably, convertibility of sterling was withdrawn.

These events – especially those relating to international finance – had a major impact on the approach to economic planning. The focus could no longer be primarily domestic and, indeed, the reliability of the *Economic Survey* as a basis for planning was seriously undermined. The Treasury, moreover, suffered a setback in its endeavour to recover its pre-war importance because it had failed to predict the convertibility crisis. However, subsequent political changes, combined with the now central importance of international financial negotiations through the Organisation for European Economic Cooperation (the agency for Marshall Aid), enormously advanced the cause of the Treasury. Initially, in 1947, Sir Stafford Cripps moved from the Board of Trade to a newly created Ministry of Economic Affairs but, after a few months' existence, this was absorbed into the Treasury when Cripps became Chancellor of the Exchequer. In its brief existence the Ministry of Economic Affairs had established the Central Economic Planning Staff (CEPS). This continued to operate in the Treasury though no attempt was made to coordinate its activities with the Economic Section of the Cabinet Office which was responsible for the *Economic Survey*. Indeed, the Treasury worked skilfully to maintain its separateness by ensuring that CEPS worked to the financial year (April to April) whilst the Economic Section prepared its *Survey* on a calendar year basis.

Government efforts were now concentrated on the balance of payments and its chosen instrument was an export drive which, in many respects, was a planning exercise. It involved the establishment of priorities and the consequent direction of resources to close the external gap. It proved very successful in terms of the increase in exports (Worswick and Ady, 1952), though new research is beginning to suggest that official efforts (largely through the agency of the Board of Trade) made only a marginal contribution as compared with general forces leading to an expansion of international trade. Furthermore, the convertibility crisis appears now to have been predominantly a problem of financial adjustment rather than one stemming from a crisis in world trade (see Chapter 6). All the while, moreover, a number of purely domestic crosscurrents were gaining in strength. Rationing and controls in general were not regarded by the public as desirable elements in planning for a better Britain but as irksome and restrictive consequences of the war which should be got rid of as soon as better times allowed. Within government itself the practicalities of administering controls in peacetime became increasingly difficult and, in the process, exposed the crucial lack of any coherent and comprehensive theory of planning. Leading economic advisers began to press for greater reliance on the price mechanism, and in 1948 the Board of Trade had a 'bonfire of economic controls'.

Even before this, the mantle of planning had passed from the Board of Trade to the Treasury and in the process its nature had changed from the planning of physical resources to financial planning. After all, the complexity of peacetime as opposed to wartime needs placed financial measures to the forefront. But the issue is also one of understanding and intent. The Treasury saw financial control as being concerned with sound finance and above party politics. As such, the operation was essentially different from planning which involved prior political judgements about what ought to be achieved. It is true that the former incorporated such normative policies as progressive taxation and the maintenance of high employment, and underlying both approaches was the belief in the desirability of more centralised economic policy-making than had operated before the war. But the broad difference is clear.

Welfare expectations and policies in such areas as health, education and housing drove the government towards concern with public expenditure and away from physical resource planning; increasingly so as physical shortages gradually disappeared. For the Treasury this presented a golden opportunity to recover its traditional dominance which it had lost during the war. The danger to be avoided was inflation. Hence the emphasis was on orthodoxy and sound finance rather than on theory. In this sense, Keynes's *General Theory* may well be regarded as self-defeating in terms of its impact on political economy. Many of the prescriptions were congenial to the tight hand and narrow intelligence of the Treasury because they laid stress on fiscal policy and underwrote macroeconomic adjustment as against any form of microeconomic planning or direction. And Keynes was, after all, a Treasury man who believed in the value of fiscal control and more or less balanced budgets over the medium term.

These developments have formed a major part of a debate over whether a Keynesian revolution had occurred in the Treasury by 1947 (Booth, 1983; 1984; Peden, 1987; Rollings, 1985; Tomlinson, 1984). The details of this cannot be considered here but two observations must be made. First, it is important to guard against judging the issue within the narrow vocabulary of economic theory. The use of some Keynesian terms by Treasury officials does not imply the acceptance of Keynes's precepts. To assume so would be seriously to underestimate the ability of civil servants to use the rhetoric of Keynesianism when it suited them and to ignore it when it did not. A good example of this is provided by the tactics of Treasury officials in the preparation of the 1947 autumn budget (Rollings, 1985). Secondly, Keynesianism is a vague term. Keynes's economics as perceived by policy-makers, or would-be policy-makers, admits of a variety of interpretations. And when we come to review the whole period we shall need to consider whether, even in the very broadest terms of demand management, Keynesianism is akin to the nineteenth-century gold standard in that it was something of universal belief but of very limited practical impact.

The haphazard nature of policy decisions is exemplified by the manner of the 30 per cent devaluation of the pound in 1949 (Cairncross and Eichengreen, 1983). Within the government political judgements on the issue were somewhat confused – Cripps, in particular, saw devaluation 'as an act of foreign policy quite as much as of economic policy' (ibid, *141*); and the final decision was made by three junior ministers outside the Cabinet. It is, moreover, an irony that these ministers (Gaitskell, Jay, Wilson) were at the same time preparing a Full Employment Bill which assumed a major capacity for planning within the government machine. So far as the economic aspects of devaluation were concerned, the situation was almost bizarre: there was little understanding of the interaction between devaluation and various parts of domestic economic policy, no careful or considered analysis of the appropriate rate, and no perception of how sterling fitted into the international structure of exchange rates or, more immediately, whether the problem stemmed from the weakness of sterling or the strength of the dollar (see Chapter 6).

On the industrial front, the translation of Cripps to the Treasury spelt the demise of regional policy as a major means of planning (Brown, 1972). Moreover, the pressure for regional aid was reduced by the effect of the export drive which stimulated even older industrial areas facing long-term decline and gave them the appearance of recovery. Quite separately, the monopolies legislation of 1948, with its general if vague aim of ensuring a 'fair' degree of competition outside the nationalised industries, implied acceptance of the operation of private enterprise in ways which were substantially inconsistent with the extension of industrial planning. But at all events the insurmountable obstacle to such planning was the total unwillingness of unions to accept manpower planning which had been at the heart of wartime economic direction. British trade unionism had found itself again after the traumas of the interwar years; and it would have nothing to do with new-fangled ideas of socialist planning. Free collective bargaining was its watchword.

During the post-war period, therefore, there was widening dichotomy between a desire for central planning and the pressures for decontrol and a return to a free market. The crises of 1947 and 1949 might have given strong impetus to planning. Instead, they provided excellent opportunities for industrial vested interest groups and, within government, the Treasury, to regain their traditional roles. Throughout the post-war period the case for a high degree of centralised planning was weakening because there was no serious attempt to address the problem of an allocative mechanism which did not give free reign to market prices and collective bargaining. There was no attempt to come to terms with the central issue of wage determination: an issue commented upon at the time but one whose importance was to become far clearer in hindsight to politicians and economists alike (Meade, 1982). Politically, any alternative would obviously have been extremely difficult to implement, while among the economists in the Economic Section the allure of Keynesian economics easily distracted attention from microeconomic problems and the need to understand how economic institutions actually worked.

The achievement of substantial economic recovery by 1950, in conjunction with a firm commitment to an international role for Britain, laid the basis (some would claim) for the consensus political economy of 'Butskellism' (Brittan, 1971; Schonfield, 1959). The tide turned against the Labour government in its marginal defeat in 1951 because of what was seen to be its still strong commitment to state regulation and control and because of the new-found attractiveness of the free-market ideology offered by the Conservatives. In truth the development of the new synthesis of the 'mixed economy' owed as much to socialist as to Tory intellectuals (Crosland, 1956). The fact that important elements in the Labour Party were thinking in these terms marked a major shift from the ideals expressed in the party's 1945 election manifesto, *Let Us Face The Future*: '[we shall] plan from the ground up, giving an appropriate place to constructive enterprise and private endeavour in the national plan'. Such ideals were grandiose both in their conception and in relation to the practicalities of post-war reconstruction. But the idea of the mixed economy was hardly less grandiose. Whilst it amounted to an important general statement on the limits of state action in a democratic society, it provided no clear basis for specific government economic action. Yet there was a crucial need for such action because the years of recovery between 1945 and 1951 had not solved major, underlying problems in the British economy. Indeed, those writers who give the Labour governments of those years high marks for achievement, fail to take sufficient account of the manner and nature of the achievement (Cairncross, 1985; Morgan, 1984). To allow the restoration of the Treasury to the position of the all-powerful policy-making body was to prove to be the Labour government's biggest and most costly mistake. The precise nature of these underlying problems and the manner in which the policies of 1945–51 relate to them, will be discussed in the chapters which follow.

3

Industry: too few producers?

Over recent years the most popular explanation of Britain's comparatively weak economic performance – and one which focuses mainly on the period of rapid decline since 1960 – has been that insufficient resources have been devoted to those parts of the economy which produce a 'marketable output' (Bacon and Eltis, 1974; Eltis, 1979). Largely, though not exclusively, these are manufacturing, mining, construction and agriculture. These activities, so it is claimed, generate the wealth on which the remainder – broadly the service sector – depends for its existence. A related analysis concentrates more narrowly on the decline in employment in the manufacturing sector over the 1970s against a background of low growth, inflation and rising unemployment (Singh, 1977). Behind the old ogre of unemployment stands a new one; and it goes by the suitably ugly name of de-industrialisation (Blackaby, 1978).

This chapter will examine the evidence on the performance of British industry against the background of these changes. There certainly does appear to be a *prima facie* case to answer.

(i) Output and employment

Table VII sets out the core facts of industrial performance. British industry's rates of growth were markedly below those of its European counterparts and as a result an absolute advantage was transformed into an absolute disadvantage over the period. The figures for productivity are probably somewhat optimistic since alternative estimates indicate no acceleration until towards the end of the period.

Table VII UK comparative growth of industrial output 1955–73 (average percentage growth per annum)

(i) Overall output growth

	UK 1955–60	1960–4	1964–9	1969–73	EEC FIVE[a] 1955–60	1960–4	1964–9	1969–73
Agriculture, forestry and fishing	3.1	3.1	1.3	4.0	2.3	1.9	1.7	1.4
Mining and quarrying	−2.9	0.4	−3.7	−2.8	0.8	0.9	−0.7	1.8
Manufacturing	2.9	3.3	3.2	2.8	6.9	6.6	6.5	5.4
Electricity, gas and water	4.6	5.6	5.2	5.2	8.8	7.3	8.1	10.0
Construction	3.1	4.5	2.3	1.3	5.6	7.1	4.3	2.4
Industrial production	2.6	3.4	2.8	2.6	6.4	6.5	6.0	5.1

(ii) Output per person

	UK 1955–60	1960–4	1964–9	1969–73	EEC FIVE[a] 1955–60	1960–4	1964–9	1969–73
Agriculture, forestry and fishing	5.0	6.0	5.7	7.1	6.1	7.4	6.1	6.3
Mining and quarrying	0.1	4.4	4.2	1.8	2.6	4.6	5.9	5.2
Manufacturing	2.2	3.2	3.4	4.4	4.1	5.5	6.3	4.7
Electricity, gas and water	4.9	3.5	5.5	8.7	6.8	6.6	9.1	9.6
Construction	2.2	1.6	2.7	0.4	2.3	3.2	4.3	2.9
Industrial production	2.2	3.1	3.5	3.9	3.7	5.0	6.1	4.7

[a] Belgium, France, Germany, Italy, Netherlands.

(iii) Gross value added per person employed in manufacturing in 1970 (UK = 100)

	UK	Belgium	France	Germany	Italy	Netherlands
At purchasing power parity exchange rates	100	155	164	155	105	183
At official exchange rates	100	160	177	176	111	182

Source: (Jones, 1976, 73, 80, 82)

Table VIII *Employment trends in industry 1950–75 (index of total number employed. 1965 = 100. % share of total working population)*

	1950 Index	1950 %	1965 Index	1965 %	1975 Index	1975 %
Agriculture, forestry and fishing	254	5.6	100	1.9	81	1.6
Mining and quarrying	135	3.7	100	2.4	56	1.4
Manufacturing	90	36.5	100	34.5	82	28.9
Food, drink and tobacco	98	3.6	100	3.2	87	2.8
Chemicals and allied industries	91	2.1	100	2.0	83	1.7
Metal manufacture	86	2.4	100	2.4	79	2.0
Mechanical engineering	67	4.0	100	5.3	73	4.0
Electrical engineering	64	2.5	100	3.4	87	3.1
Shipbuilding and marine engineering	140	1.3	100	0.8	84	0.7
Vehicles	117	4.4	100	3.3	87	3.0
Metal goods, other	85	2.2	100	2.3	92	2.1
Textiles	124	4.4	100	3.1	65	2.1
Leather, leather goods, fur	131	0.3	100	0.2	69	0.1
Clothing and footwear	126	3.1	100	2.1	72	1.6
Bricks, pottery, glass, cement	92	1.4	100	1.4	77	1.1
Timber, furniture	106	1.4	100	1.2	88	1.1
Paper, printing, publishing	81	2.3	100	2.5	88	2.2
Other	76	1.1	100	1.3	99	1.3
Construction	90	6.6	100	6.5	77	5.2
Gas, electricity, water	92	1.7	100	1.6	84	1.4
Transport and communication	174	12.5	100	6.4	92	6.0
Total employment for the whole economy	88		100		95	

Source: Derived from *Employment Gazette.*

For present purposes these data need to be sub-divided a little more in terms of labour supply and capital investment. The employment trends are given in Table VIII. The overall and accelerating decline in the manufacturing sector and its sub-groups from the mid 1960s stands out. One difference occurs in relation to the longer term in that shipbuilding, textiles, clothing and footwear, motor vehicles, timber and furniture, leather and fur, had already declined from their 1950 position by 1964. Correspondingly, a group of industries – including chemicals, electrical engineering, mechanical engineering, building supplies, pottery, glass, paper, printing, publishing – had experienced considerable growth in employment. Of the other sectors, construction and gas, electricity and water had increased whilst agriculture, mining and transport showed substantial falls.

These trends have to be placed within the broader framework of changes in the total labour force. The rate of growth of total working population fell to zero by the mid 1960s. This was the outcome of changes in population growth and its age distribution which were only partly compensated for by the marked increase in female participation ratios, especially of those in the 25–60 age groups (Matthews *et al.*, 1982). Moreover, the large element of part-time female employment was very responsive to any downward demand pressure (Prest and Coppock, various edns). If the labour supply is refined further to the level of labour input, which takes account of the length of the working year, then zero growth is recorded from 1951; and from the mid 1960s it turned into an actual decline at over 1 per cent per annum. The over-riding reason for the fall was the reduction in the working week which was particularly marked from 1966 onwards and was disproportionately large among female workers who were constituting a bigger share of the total working population. None of these calculations takes account of the elusive element of changes in the quality of labour. Extremely crude estimates suggest some improvement over the post-war period (Matthews *et al.*, 1982). At all events, it is difficult to see how such a gain would do more than very marginally modify the picture which has been outlined.

The upshot that was the share of manufacturing industry in employment was 36% in 1960, 35% in 1970 and 31% in 1975. Changes in the other sectors of industry were more marked. Within this overall decline there was a steady structural shift from traditional staple industries to the more buoyant ones as measured by international demand. It is noticeable, however, that the shift came nowhere near eradicating disparities in regional employment opportunities which were heavily influenced by the high degree of concentration of the old staple industries: thus, at the extremes, unemployment in London and the South-East was 56% of the UK rate in 1973 and in the North 174%. In Wales the rate was 130%

Table IX *Gross fixed capital formation per head of employed labour force in manufacturing – UK compared 1965–75*

	(Current US $ and exchange rates UK = 100)		
	1965	1970	1975
United Kingdom	100	100	100
Belgium	168	203	257
France[a]	197	238	267
Germany[b]	–	–	186[d]
Italy[a]	80	124	160[d]
Netherlands[a]	170	270	309
Japan	100	218	176
Sweden	167	200	292
USA[c]	365	355	293

Source: (Blackaby, 1979, *247*).
[a] Plus other industrial sectors.
[b] Production industries excluding quarrying and mining.
[c] Manufacturing employment estimated.
[d] 1974.

of the UK average, in Scotland 170%, in Northern Ireland 237% and in the North-West 133% (Matthews *et al.*, 1982).

(ii) Investment

The investment record for the period is best placed within an international context. The figures shown in Table IX are broadly representative. Once again, post-war performance was significantly above the level for the interwar years, but in international terms it was substantially below par. Interpretation of these data is far from straightforward, however. Whilst there is wide agreement that investment is a necessary condition of economic growth and that within fairly wide margins higher levels of performance require higher levels of investment, the direction of this relationship cannot be conclusively demonstrated; it may well be the case that the two occur together. Account also has to be taken of the distribution of investment between branches of industry and of the intensity and efficiency of capital use – though the latter is extremely difficult to measure. What is more, on an international comparative basis the level of investment in relation to the achieved rate of growth was not low in the UK – indeed, it was on average three times the German level over the late 1960s and early 1970s (Cairncross *et al.*, 1977; Williams, 1962). Hence, explanations and prescriptions which stress higher investment as the direct means to higher growth in the UK are probably very wide of the mark (Pollard, 1982).

The claim is sometimes made that the capacity of British industry to achieve higher absolute levels of investment has been weakened by declining rates of profit (Flemming *et al.*, 1976). In addition, low profits might be assumed to have lowered expectations of future profits and hence weakened the incentive to invest – a factor shown by the Radcliffe Report (1959) to have been far more important in determining investment policy than the rate of interest. On the face of it gross profit rates showed a steady decline over the 1960s and a dramatic fall between 1970 and 1975 from 23 per cent to 13 per cent; if capital consumption is taken into account the fall was from 17 to 4 per cent. On a number of grounds, however, these statistics are misleading for private and, in particular, nationalised industry. The figures make no allowance for investment grants, special depreciation allowances, and accounting devices which were used to reap rewards in the form of capital gains (which have been less highly taxed) instead of trading profits (King, 1975).

Furthermore, it is not the case that UK corporation tax rates were particularly unfavourable in international terms (Kay and King, 1978). Like all British direct taxation, as the absolute level of profits increases the tax loses its progressiveness and becomes a flat rate (Caves and Krause, 1980). Another factor to be taken into account is the form and associated cost of corporate finance. Early evidence indicates a marked shift over the 1970s to monetised finance in the form of capital leasing by manufacturing industry from financial institutions with a corresponding decline in primary capital markets (Rybczynski, 1982). Whether this simply amounts to short-term cost-effectiveness in the face of declining markets rather than more general efficient use of resources is not clear.

There are further enormous complications in the case of nationalised industries. Analyses of a number of them have drawn attention to government constraints on investment through holding down prices (Ashworth, 1986), imposing unfavourable borrowing terms and, in some cases, outright refusal to sanction borrowing (Pryke, 1981). But it is difficult to see these factors as amounting to an absolute restriction when put against the equally well recorded government support for overcapacity and inefficient working. In sum, the general impression to be gained from the literature is that industrial profits were slimmed over the period, but by nothing like as much as bald balance sheet figures suggest, and that an easing in the cost of finance over the 1960s was followed by a hardening in the early 1970s. There still remains the problem of cause and effect. Why should uncompetitive and low-productivity industry have yielded other than low profit rates?

(iii) Productivity

A number of studies demonstrate that Britain's lower productivity performance in international terms cannot be attributed to a substantially disproportionate concentration of labour in particular industries (Panic, 1976). It is somewhat paradoxical that structural shift does not appear to have been a major factor in productivity growth after the war, because it is well known that structural imbalances contributed substantially to unemployment between the wars. In part, the resolution of the paradox is almost certainly in terms of the accuracy of the available data. In larger part, however, it probably lies with matters of definition. If types of industry could be defined more sharply then it seems likely that although by 1970 British industry matched the international pattern, this had occurred as a result of some substantial relative shifts in employment in the UK over the 1950s and 1960s. An obvious example is the switch from cotton to artificial fibres within the textile industry.

Concentration in the literature on productivity growth tends to deflect attention from absolute differences in productivity. Thus, while the USA has shared the distinction of a comparatively low overall growth rate with the UK in the post-war period, the level of its labour productivity in manufacturing industry has consistently been 50 per cent higher than the UK (Caves and Krause, 1980).

Similarly, in relation to a whole range of competitors, studies of particular industries tell the same story; Britain's labour costs per hour were low but when these are translated into labour costs per unit of output the reverse is the case (Kravis, 1976; Pratten, 1976b; Ray, 1976). The underlying reasons for this will be considered more fully below but in general it seems clear that large, volume-production industries were characterised by low throughput per worker because of over-manning and insufficient intensity of capital use (Bacon and Eltis, 1974; Pratten, 1971, 1976a). By contrast, higher labour costs per hour among overseas competitors represented higher income levels which were the consequence of higher productivity (Ray, 1976). These relationships are particularly important since some writers present comparatively low absolute wage levels in the UK as a competitive advantage instead of as a penalty for overall poor performance (Williams *et al.*, 1983).

Given low absolute levels of productivity, Britain's accelerated productivity growth over the post-war period might well appear as something of an easy success. Confirmation of this view is provided by the enormous and extremely rapid gains in productivity which were achieved in the motor vehicle and iron and steel industries when they came under strong pressure through government rationalisation schemes in the 1970s (Bhaskar, 1979). Even more, the thesis that the economy has suffered from too few producers in the manufacturing sector rings very hollow indeed (Kaldor, 1966, 1968, 1975). If manufacturing employment had remained at the 1966 level until 1974 then output would have been higher by 8.6 per cent; but if Britain had matched French or German growth in output per man hour since 1958 then even with the reduction in the labour force the 1974 output level would have been higher by no less than 70 per cent (Gomulka, 1979). Correspondingly, factor input analysis, which identifies the labour force as the main constraint on growth, begs the fundamental question of its absolute level of productivity.

There is another apparent paradox between Britain's comparatively poor level of productivity and the fact that manufacturing's share of GDP is much the same as for other major economies. It is explained by the slow growth of GDP in the UK; consequently, comparisons of GDP per head place Britain in a very lowly position.

More difficult to judge is the impact of productivity growth on

Table X *Industrial import penetration of UK domestic market 1961–75 (imports as % domestic sales)*

	Total imports	Remaining imports		Total imports	Remaining imports
1961	11	10	1968	17	15
1962	11	9	1969	18	14
1963	11	10	1970	18	15
1964	14	12	1971	18	15
1965	13	11	1972	21	18
1966	14	12	1973	25	22
1967	15	12	1974	31	28
			1975	28	25

Source: (Bacon and Eltis, 1976, *217–31*).
Remaining imports = less import content of exports.

the size of the labour force. The proportion in manufacturing was not out of line in international terms up to the early 1970s. Moreover, as has been noted, by the early 1970s the structure of British industry was similar to that of the EEC countries as measured by the *proportionate* distribution of employment. For advanced economies, substantial changes had occurred over the latter half of the 1960s because of loss of comparative advantage in what had become basic technologies which could be mastered by low-income countries, together with changes in the nature of world demand and direct and indirect forms of trade barriers erected to protect domestic industry. But there are grounds for arguing that in the UK case a considerably better productivity record would have resulted in a smaller *absolute* fall. It is crucial to the case that account is taken of something which is obscured by straightforward relative comparisons between countries around 1970. Between 1960 and the early 1970s the share of manufacturing industry in employment in Britain decreased and the *total* labour force itself declined from the mid 1960s. In Germany, France and Japan the opposite was broadly the case. And since international competition in manufacturing is substantially dependent on comparable scales of production, it can be argued that, in absolute terms, by the early 1970s there were too few workers in British industry, especially in those involving advanced technology. There are reasons, therefore, why Britain might be expected to have had a somewhat higher than average share of its workforce in manufacturing industry. The crucial assumption underlying this analysis, in contrast to those which have focused on the rate of growth of labour supply and the idea of too few producers, is that the achievement of higher productivity is a *prior condition* for and not a *consequence* of a higher rate of growth of the manufacturing labour force (cf. Kaldor, 1966, 1968, 1975; Bacon and Eltis, 1974; Eltis, 1979).

(iv) Competitiveness

Productivity growth and competitiveness are vitally linked though the relationship is a complex one. One measure of it is the degree of import penetration (Table X). Numerous analyses leave no doubt that the scale of these changes cannot be explained by any combination of relative adjustments within the context of post-war international economic recovery, the emergence of new industrial nations, the vigorous operation of comparative advantage within a high growth of trade, or by the substantial increase in semi-manufactures (Panic, 1975). The extent of import penetration amounts to a serious decline in Britain's competitive position. The average income elasticity of demand for imports was of the order of 1.5 to 2.0 between the late 1950s and the early 1970s, but this obscures quite wide variations between goods and there are strong grounds for believing that in expansionary phases the ratio rose to as high as 5.0 or 6.0; and even the average for manufactured goods was just over 3.0 (Eltis, 1979). An income elasticity of demand for imports which was higher than the corresponding change in foreign demand for British goods imposed a serious balance of payments constraint because of the requirement to maintain a fixed exchange rate. Consequently, Britain had to hold its overall growth at a correspondingly proportionate level below the growth of its leading competitors (Thirwall, 1982). The alternative was an unsustainable loss of financial reserves. A whole range of industries were affected but among the more striking examples were motor vehicles. In 1965 only 5 per cent of demand was met by imports, by 1970 it was 14 per cent rising to 33 per cent by 1975 and to a staggering 60 per cent by the early 1980s (Wells and Imber, 1977;

Williams *et al.*, 1983). Various branches of the electronics industry provide equally dramatic examples. Quite simply, domestic industry's performance was not sufficiently competitive to match a high level of domestic demand.

Estimates of the expected share of British exports of manufactures in world trade are necessarily crude but a conservative one puts it at just over 11.0 per cent in 1975 as against an actual 9 per cent (Batchelor *et al.*, 1980; Panic, 1975). Had 11.0 per cent been achieved in 1975, it would have transformed Britain's balance of payments and turned a substantial negative current balance for that year into a modest surplus.

So why has the performance of manufacturing industry fallen so dangerously low? The decline is not directly attributable to the structure of trade: in broad terms, at least, Britain has had as large a share in the growth sectors of world trade as her competitors (Batchelor *et al.*, 1980; Prest and Coppock, various edns). Some commentators have gone further and pointed to the relatively high proportion of UK production which has been exported and to the high ratio of exports of GDP in international terms. But this is a somewhat misleading comparison since it takes no account of the relatively low absolute level of British GDP per head combined with the fact that non-traded goods become a proportionately larger share at higher levels of income. There remains, nevertheless, the problem of precisely what is meant by lack of competitiveness.

The obvious starting point is price. On this measure, in average terms, Britain was not at a disadvantage after 1967 since exchange rate adjustments compensated for higher costs (National Institute, 1972). This has led some economists to rule out or substantially to downgrade price as a factor (Caves, 1968; Posner and Steer, 1979). But such judgements are questionable because they rely on composite time series of export prices which do not expose variations in the pattern and timing of price changes of individual goods. Although much more work needs to be done in this area, the impression gained by surveying a range of industries is one of foreign incursions occurring at different times with price being a significant element at certain stages. Moreover, once a foreign producer has captured what he judges to be a significant share of the market he then eases prices upwards while increasing his share by other devices such as advertising and superior servicing and distribution. The crunch comes for domestic producers because in the real world economic processes cannot adjust smoothly in response to reverse movements in quantifiable variables such as price so that market share cannot easily be regained. Over and above this, there were no exchange rate adjustments before 1967 by which time, anyway, much serious damage had already been done (Hughes and Thirlwall, 1977).

Much more complicated is how to make allowance for price differences which reflect different qualities of goods. The categories within which price comparisons are made, therefore, are far from homogeneous. Such differences may be identifiable ones such as workmanship and reliability. British car manufacturers built up an unenviable reputation over the late 1940s and in the 1950s in both respects (Bhaskar, 1979; Pagnamenta and Overy, 1984). More difficult to specify is product design though many examples are cited in the literature. Better foreign design may well mean no more than extra features being provided for the same price as the basic equivalent UK model (CPRS, 1975). Poor delivery dates and servicing facilities are further factors to which empirical studies have attached major, even primary importance. But still these are all proximate causes of poor performance. Why has British industry failed so comprehensively in these ways?

A major part of the explanation undoubtedly is to be found in the areas of management practices, labour relations and business organisation, which are discussed below (Chapter 5; Bacon and Eltis, 1974; Pratten, 1976b). But there are two factors which need to be highlighted here. First, Britain's position in world trade in 1950 resulted from a temporary advance since, despite enormous difficulties, she was better placed to make some immediate recovery from the effects of the world war than the devastated economies of Europe and Japan (Milward, 1984). But the value of this advantage is dubious. The over-riding aim was to export at all costs. It was a policy which reinforced traditional methods in the older sectors of industry and placed a premium on short-term production at the expense of innovative development. Iron and steel and shipbuilding are good examples of the former and motor vehicles and electrical engineering equipment of the latter. Furthermore, the policy acclimatised industry to captive markets in the form of pressing demands from foreigners for basic goods and equipment and to willing acceptance by ration-ridden domestic consumers for whom something was better than nothing. In such an environment there was little premium on design, delivery and service. Unhappily, habits which may have had some virtue in times of scarcity became vices in times of relative abundance. But how far was British industry simply a victim of circumstances?

By early 1949 the outlook was improving, yet there was a lack of will on the part of both industry and government to plan for the return to free markets at home and abroad. In particular, the government gave little attention to using its powers over investment to re-structure major sectors of industry, as was being done on the Continent and in Japan (Estrin and Holmes, 1983; Hayward and Narkiewicz, 1978). True, new elements were introduced in 1950 in the form of rearmament and the Korean war. But the demands these placed on industry were not imposed from outside but were the result of a scale of priorities which placed international responsibilities (or illusions) before domestic economic reform (Cairncross, 1985).

The second factor was the changing international structure of industrial production. Under the expansionary conditions of the 1950s, Britain's position began to slip but industries and firms were not sensitive to it because, absolutely, exports continued to grow. Underlying this other processes were at work. There was an enormous increase in world industrial capacity as the technological gap between the USA and the major economies was closed; and over the somewhat longer term, the income elasticity of demand for manufactured goods fell. These processes occurred within a pattern of international trade which was dominated by the exchange of manufactured goods for manufactured goods between the major economies. Altogether this led to an effect which might be described as a tapering of market opportunities, and it was sharpened as international growth rates decelerated in the early 1970s. Worse was to come. The impact of the oil crisis and its associated inflation led to the first actual decline in income for OECD countries for over a quarter of a century. In these conditions the weaknesses of British industry were rawly exposed to international competition. The impact was all the greater because for nearly two decades industry had benefited from particularly favourable terms of trade for raw materials and food which, in various ways, had moderated production costs and wage demands. Not surprisingly, therefore, import penetration increased from the mid 1960s onwards and then moved at an alarming rate in the early 1970s. Seen in this light de-industrialisation was not the onset of a foreign disease but the unavoidable expiation of past neglect.

One area of neglect which has not been touched upon is expenditure on research and development. Only rough and ready figures are available because of problems of definition. In broad terms these show Britain riding high in the international league table in the 1950s and 1960s but falling heavily over the 1970s (Freeman, 1979). Of course, this tells us nothing about the effectiveness of these efforts. Attempts have been made to relate expenditure on R and D to performance indicators both in aggregate terms and at the level of particular industries (Pavitt, 1980). Immediately, however, this raises the problem of collinearity; added to which, no really strong pattern emerges apart from some significant relationship between research and development expenditure and export performance among most, though not all, capital goods industries.

Perhaps more revealing is the evidence on sources and distribution of research funds which proved to be highly related. In the UK the government provided nearly 50 per cent of the funding, which compared well with other countries. The crucial difference, however, is that over half of this amount went on defence (which is comparable to the USA) whereas in the EEC the proportion was one-quarter and in Japan zero. Moreover, the commercial spin-off from defence research has proved to be nothing like as great as the gains made from comparable expenditures on industrial research (Peck, 1968). Similarly, the UK has committed a disproportionate amount of expenditure to basic research (absorbing something like 12 per cent of professional scientific manpower). Thus Britain has committed heavy expenditures to just those areas in which she is at a massive comparative disadvantage against the USA. The aircraft industry alone accounted for one-third of expenditure. The achievements are well recorded: the Brabazon airliner, the abortive TSR2 fighter plane and Concorde – the fastest white elephant of modern times.

Expenditure on R and D is just part of the broader process of innovation and technological change which incorporates a number of other elements (Gomulka, 1979). To begin with, there is 'learning by doing' which frequently involves relatively quite small alterations in techniques and/or practices but which, cumulatively, can add up to major productivity gains. Secondly, technical innovation may occur directly in the factory or workshop without any prior research expenditure and possibly as pure serendipity. Spectacular examples of this are rayon and float glass. The remaining three elements are variants of benefiting from technical advances made abroad. Benefits can occur directly through licences or patents, indirectly by means of free scientific knowledge or industrial espionage, or by acquisition through the purchase of machines or through foreign investment. Some commentators see the last group mainly in terms of the process of the diffusion of technology, but this would seem to be too narrow a use of the concept since spread or diffusion is an essential, and probably the most important, element in all forms of technological change. There is substantial evidence in the literature already cited that it has been the critical area of failure in Britain. Whereas there are examples of best practice technology efficiently applied throughout British industry, they are far from sufficiently diffused to match international competition.

To recognise the failure is only to raise, once again, the question of why it was so? At this point the literature of economic analysis fades into reluctant acceptance of the answer having to be sought in social, cultural and political attitudes and relationships, elements which are not susceptible to quantitative techniques (Carter, 1981). The economic historian's approach to these matters will be considered below (Chapters 5, 7, 8).

(v) Nationalised industry and agriculture

A large segment of British industry since the war has been publicly owned. It includes coal, gas, electricity, civil aviation, railways, the Post Office and, since 1967, steel. Its share of total industrial activity has varied over the period but the figures for the late 1960s are representative. These show public industry to have accounted for 11 per cent of GDP, not far short of 10 per cent of the workforce and a level of investment equivalent to the whole of private manufacturing (Prest and Coppock, 1983). Evaluation of its performance is hazardous because it has not generally been subject to commercial practices and norms (Pryke, 1981). In the case of British Rail, for example, large subsidies have been provided to sustain a degree of social service in what would otherwise be uneconomic provisions. Furthermore, all publicly owned industries have, not surprisingly, proved vulnerable to ministerial interference dictated by short-term political expediency (Ashworth, 1986; Hannah, 1982). To make matters worse, the monopolistic character of the sector has been blatantly exploited by trade unions, though over the longer run this has probably resulted in major job losses since most of the industries are subject to competition in the form of alternative goods. For example, over the period rail transport lost heavily to road transport (though assessment is complicated by problems of whether road transport paid the full costs of its operation) and more recently coal has lost to alternative forms of energy supply.

One attempt to assess the performance of publicly owned industries presents a picture of an average rate of growth of productivity per man very similar to private manufacture but, within that, very wide variations between a high for British Gas and a low for the National Coal Board. Likewise the same range of factors as for industry generally has led to correspondingly poor performance in international terms. But there are two further points which emerge from considerations of a wide range of literature relating to public enterprise: big investment decisions have been complicated and delayed as a result of having to be considered by a number of government departments; such decisions have been easy prey to party political pressures when they have involved the location of new plants and/or closure of old ones (Knight, 1974). To a degree this is probably inevitable in state-run industry. At the same time, however, some of these weaknesses might have been avoided if more careful attention had been given to commercial needs by those originally responsible for framing the administrative structures of nationalised industries (Chester, 1975).

Agriculture, the remaining industry to be considered, presents the paradox of being subjected to an enormous apparatus of state regulation while landowners have remained firmly among the leading cadres of the Tory Party. From an initial position of advantage in immediate post-war Britain – when food was required almost at any cost – the agricultural interest succeeded in capturing the regulatory mechanism through the exercise of highly successful pressure-group politics. In narrower economic terms agriculture provides a striking example of how misleading bald figures for labour productivity can be. Ostensibly agriculture has a fine record – between 1961 and 1973 labour productivity bounded along at over 7 per cent per annum though overall growth of output at just under 3 per cent was less impressive (Matthews *et al.*, 1982). This was achieved, however, on the basis of enormous subsidies – both direct in the form of support prices and indirect in the form of a whole range of grants and allowances – which sustained a high-cost agriculture when judged in international terms. By the early 1970s, direct subsidies at just under £400m were not far short of the equivalent of half all central and local government expenditure on roads and public highways; and the pattern has been intensified under the agricultural policy of the EEC since 1973. By the early 1950s the claim that agriculture saved valuable foreign exchange was already paper-thin. And even if the case for agriculture is extended to include welfare considerations concerned with the preservation of rural life (and such claims have regularly been made by the agricultural interest) then the creation of mini-prairies and suburbanised villages would testify to its failure. In short, if agriculture is judged by the criteria of performance applied to manufacturing industry, there is every reason to argue that its output has been artificially and substantially inflated for the whole period since 1950. Given its size – in terms of employment it was equivalent, for example, to either mining or chemicals in the early 1970s – this represented a serious loss of resources to other sectors of the economy.

(vi) Too few producers?

The popular appeal of 'Too Few Producers' to explain Britain's weak economic performance is understandable. It makes for easy division of the labour force into 'essential' and 'inessential' workers, and thus avoids the need to consider whether there is any degree of essential interdependence between them. At the level of political debate the message has also proved widely attractive, though with the qualification that whilst the political right has tended to adopt the common form, the left has preferred the more acute form of de-industrialisation. The reason for this difference is probably that the one wishes to justify cuts in welfare expenditure whereas the other is aiming for more direct state control of industry. Whatever the reason, however, our examination of the evidence gives little support for either thesis.

The decline in employment in manufacturing industry, in both absolute terms and as a proportion of the labour force, is clear enough. But the broad UK pattern is by no means unusual in comparison with other major economies. The big differences are to be measured in terms of rates of growth of output and of levels of output per head. When these indicators are examined in more detail in relation to investment, productivity and competitiveness, the picture which emerges is not predominantly one of inadequate supplies of labour in manufacturing industry but one of the low productive efficiency of the existing labour force as it is employed in combination with other factors of production. There is, of course, always the problem in economic analysis of interpreting the dynamic relationships between factors of production. Thus there is an implication in some analyses that an increase in the supply of labour to manufacturing industry would lead to higher levels of productivity and rates of output growth. The evidence surveyed above, however, suggests that such gains would not occur. Low productivity (often the result of too much labour through over-manning) has led to poor competitiveness, market failure and the inevitable contraction of industry. The cry of 'Too Few Producers' results from a confusion of cause and effect.

To demonstrate that in the UK the relationship runs from low productivity to poor competitiveness is one thing. To explain why it does so is quite another matter. The foregoing discussion has dealt with proximate causes. Subsequent chapters will examine the evidence relating to the more fundamental elements at work. Before doing so, however, it is necessary to look at that sector of the economy which, according to some, harbours the lotus eaters of post-war Britain, namely, services.

4
The service industries

For the economic historian, as for the economist, services constitute the most enigmatic sector of the economy. It is amorphous in composition and much of its capital is intangible. But it is large. If it is taken to include distribution, financial and business services, government and a whole range of what are defined as miscellaneous services – which incorporate such disparate occupations as garage mechanics and actors – the sector accounted for just under half the labour force and a similar share of output by the early 1970s. Between 1950 and the early 1970s the sector grew by just under 10 per cent and the increase was mainly made up of financial and commercial services. Within the period, however, there were some changes in employment patterns, the most important features being a swing in government services from 7 per cent to 6 per cent in the early 1960s and then back again by the end of the period, and an almost obverse swing in distribution from 11 to 13 per cent and back to 12 per cent. The main features are shown in Table XI.

Any calculation of output growth is necessarily on a very broad base. For the whole sector it is much in line with the overall growth of GDP, but it is noteworthy that between 1951 and 1964 insurance, and banking and finance grew by nearly 50 per cent faster than GDP and between 1964 and 1973 by just over 90 per cent (Matthews *et al.*, 1982). The balancing slower growth was supplied by the portmanteau of miscellaneous services. Measures of productivity growth are even cruder and can be made only in terms of labour productivity. Moreover, it is necessary to remember that overall productivity will be affected by the pattern of demand for services (because they vary in terms of their potential

Table XI *Employment trends in services 1950–75 (index of total number employed 1965 = 100. % share of total working population)*

	1950		1965		1975	
	Index	%	Index	%	Index	%
Distributive trades	71	12.2	100	12.8	90	12.2
Insurance, banking, finance	67	2.5	100	2.7	169	4.9
Professional and scientific	59	8.2	100	10.3	144	15.7
Miscellaneous services	76	9.8	100	9.4	97	9.7
Public administration	105	8.0	100	5.7	122	7.3
(National government service)	(115)	(3.7)	(100)	(2.4)	(113)	(2.9)
(Local government service)	(97)	(4.3)	(100)	(3.3)	(129)	(4.4)
Overall index: total %	74	40.7	100	40.9	115	49.8

Source: Annual Abstract of Statistics.

labour productivity) as well as by the efficiency with which they are supplied. Whilst there are no satisfactory measures of capital stock for this sector its capital needs are large and include a substantial proportion of the real but elusive element of human capital. There are, nevertheless, some interesting contrasts. Between 1951 and 1964 productivity of the miscellaneous services group was growing at 3.4 per cent per annum as against 2.8 per cent for the whole economy, 2.1 per cent for insurance, banking and finance and 1.7 per cent for the distributive trades. In the subsequent period up to 1973 when the rate for the whole economy was 3.7 per cent, the distributive services shot ahead to 4.5 per cent whereas the financial sector trailed at 2.9 per cent and miscellaneous services limped behind at 1.5 per cent. It is far from clear how to interpret this, however. Certainly the performance of distribution reflected a marked change in retailing with the rapid growth in supermarkets and the decline of small and some specialist retailers resulting in a big shake-out of labour. For the remainder, the average figures equally certainly obscure wide variations.

The sheer scale of the service sector has made it the focus for attack by the proponents of the de-industrialisation thesis. In particular employment in central and local government has come under fierce assault because of its non-market nature. In total numbers the army of officialdom increased from 1.3m to 1.7m between 1960 and 1975 (Bacon and Eltis, 1974; Eltis, 1979). But this increase was minuscule when set against the potential gain from an improvement in industrial productivity which would make up only half the gap between Britain and its competitors. Added to which, the UK was by no means out of line internationally in terms of the proportion of employees in the public sector. Even more important, major services play an essential role in conditioning the quality of labour in the so-called market sector. The question then is not one of the balance of quantities between 'market' and 'non-market' activities, but of the quality of performance of such services which vitally inter-relate with more directly market-determined employment. Because of the multifarious nature of the sector our survey is necessarily selective; and the case of government service is dealt with later in the context of policy formation (Chapter 7).

Education is a large and important example. Much criticism has been levelled at the nature of the upper reaches of the English educational system before 1914, with its emphasis on liberal studies within the ethos of the public school which extolled the virtues of the gentleman amateur (Coleman, 1973). If nothing else, the system helped to ensure that incompetence – even failure – would be achieved nobly in later life. All of which was so different from the manner in which education was treated by Britain's rising industrial competitors such as Germany, Japan and even France (Locke, 1984). Whilst the form and degree of criticism has changed over the twentieth century, in essence it has remained the same, with similar international contrasts being drawn. The famous Education Act of 1944 extended educational opportunity but did little to alter the nature of it. The enormous expansion of higher education since 1960 has arguably provided a further extension of opportunity, but it has not succeeded in developing parity of esteem with universities for institutions supposed to be concentrating on vocational and technical education – an aspect which, once again, has invited numerous international comparisons (Postan, 1967; Robbins, 1963).

Shortages of skilled manpower and management skills may well be immediately traceable to these developments but they are not, by any means, wholly attributable to them. On the one hand, the narrowly hierarchical nature of British education and the vested interests in maintaining it have undoubtedly been powerful forces at work (Barnett, 1986). On the other hand, the system has been strongly conditioned by pressures and demands placed upon it. Social and cultural values have clearly been different in Britain from those in, say, Germany or the USA. Explanations of this in terms of 'class interest' appear simplistic to an extreme degree. These values are the result of several causes and are inter-related with the system of education. Correspondingly, business histories and more general industrial studies provide much evidence of the lack of demand from the top for new forms of education and resistance from organised labour below to alterations in traditional methods of training and recruitment (Coleman, 1980).

The economic effects of a service such as education are clearly impossible to quantify accurately, and attempts by economists to calculate returns on investment in education are laden with many assumptions and are unavoidably narrow in approach; in particular, the financial return is calculated on the basis of a ratio between income and the cost of educational qualifications (Blaug, 1965; Morris and Ziderman, 1971). Likewise, the agencies of central and local government necessarily have a powerful effect, both directly and indirectly, on industrial performance. But measurement of the effect is even more difficult than in the case of education. Therefore, much more work needs to be done by economic and social historians in these fields before any conclusions can be drawn. There is much to suggest, yet little to confirm, that poor performance in these areas has played a crucial part in affecting the overall performance of the economy. Clearly, the category of social services is obviously too wide to base investigation upon since some of its elements may well be things which only rich societies can afford. It is equally true, however, that other of its elements are important means to the attainment of these riches.

One area for which it is possible to offer some qualitative assessment of performance is financial and commercial services. With the expansion of employment went a rapid rise in the financial turnover and growth in importance of particular types of financial institutions (Table XII). These changes were obviously directly related to rising real income but they resulted, also, from the system of taxation (Kay and King, 1978). Thus, for private individuals there were considerable incentives to holding wealth in the form of dwellings and various forms of insurance which, as well, involved substantial investments in property and land. Corre-

Table XII *Total holdings of financial institutions 1938–72 (£m) (at 1972 prices)*

	1938	1952	1962	1963	1972
Insurance companies	8,535	8,256	13,162	17,350	22,230
Pension funds	2,453	2,580	6,726	8,729	12,010
Investment companies	1,521	1,197	3,797	5,470	7,520
Unit trusts	392	2,064	418	1,078	2,550

Source: Prais, 1976, *116*.

spondingly, much energy and skill was concentrated on promoting and reaping capital gains which, taking the period as a whole, were either untaxed or lightly taxed in sharp contrast to the taxation of income. Nevertheless, there are grounds for asking whether the measurable distribution of wealth-holding is simply a matter of choice within Britain in comparison with other leading economies, or whether the financial services sector forms the agency which actively determines that distribution rather than simply facilitating it. Even very rough comparisons show how, in other economies, investment in company securities forms a much higher proportion of personal wealth-holding than in the UK (Caves and Krause, 1980; HMSO, 1980). The crucial matter, of course, is the dynamics of the process. Hence, one obvious question is how does this pattern of wealth-holding relate to the overall level of investment and the rate of economic growth? It is worth noting that whereas profit shares in manufacturing fell over the period, in the financial sector they were maintained at a high and even rising level (Brown and Sheriff, 1978).

Against the complexity of the relationships raised here it is possible to present some hard evidence of the actual working of financial institutions. In 1931 the Macmillan Committee defined the so-called Macmillan gap, which amounted to a plea to clearing banks to provide more long-term financial assistance to manufacturing industry, especially to medium-sized firms. One section of the report compared Britain unfavourably in this regard with Germany, France and the United States. The same issues were raised before the Wilson Committee (1980) half a century later. On this occasion examination of the problem was more intense. Maybe as a result, there were considerable differences of opinion within the committee as to the nature of the relationship between finance and industry and whether it should be altered by the development of new institutional arrangements. The committee's recommendations were accordingly ambivalent. Yet the evidence presented suggested strongly that there was still a significant lack of long-term cooperation between finance and industry.

To counter-balance any shortcomings on the domestic front claims have frequently been made about the major contribution which financial services rendered to the economy through invisible exports. Ostensibly more compelling is the argument that if British manufacturing industry had matched insurance, banking, and allied financial services, in terms of international competitiveness, the economy would have been in a very healthy state indeed. Services were clearly less affected by import penetration than manufacturing; and between 1955 and 1975 their share of the world total fell from 25 to 15 per cent, which compares very favourably with the performance of manufactured goods (Sargent, 1979). From the Radcliffe Report (1959) onwards, moreover, figures have been produced to show the value of their contribution; and over the period invisible exports from the financial sector have been cast in the role of saviour of the balance of payments. Yet the invisible balance may well be a measure of weakness rather than of strength, particularly since financial services have not shown outstanding growth in productivity: as has been noted it was below that of domestic manufacturing and far below that for manufacturing among Britain's major competitors.

This somewhat more modest view of services performance is easily obscured by the claims made for their role in the balance of payments, which certainly appears impressive. Thus between 1966 and 1976 net overseas earnings rose on average by 5.3 times as against 2.3 times for manufacturing. Within this overall increase insurance grew by a factor of 11.7, construction overseas by 11.4, banking by 7.7, brokerage by 7.3 and commodity trading by 5.8. Indeed, the average was pulled down by lumpy short-term payments made to help finance the early development of North Sea oil (Sargent, 1979). Insurance, banking, finance and allied services showed up well, also, on a broader basis. In 1976, for example, they returned a gross GDP per person employed of £6,530 as against £4,140 for manufacturing. Taken together, however, these figures mean no more and no less than services managing to expand rapidly enough to maintain their overall world share whereas manufacturing steadily dropped way behind in this race. But the really crucial point is that although the strong international position of UK services reflected comparative advantage, it was comparative advantage in a low productivity growth sector. Put another way: it may well have paid other industrial economies to allow the UK to take in their financial washing.[1] These strictures apply specifically to financial services; an important and different case is that of tourism where the UK's world share has shown a marked improvement particularly since 1974 (ibid).

Measures of productivity in services – even within the restricted area which has just been examined – are, of course, subject to wide margins of error. Moreover, the distinction between services and manufacturing has been exaggerated over recent years by the growth of leasing (Rybczynski, 1982). By this means capital equipment employed in manufacturing is owned by the services sector. If this were allowed for in factor input analysis, the productivity of manufacturing would be shown as correspondingly lower. Moreover, services are generally less subject to cyclical fluctuations than manufacturing. But altogether, productivity has almost certainly been lower in services than in manufacturing by a significant margin and this involves a double irony: a major part of the improvement of productivity in manufacturing from the 1960s onwards resulted from a shake-out of labour much of which, in effect, found its way into the lower productivity services.

Another marked feature of the service industries is the large amount of female labour they employ: among the highest levels were professional and scientific services where it was 70 per cent by 1970 and in both catering and retailing just over 60 per cent. Part-time female labour is particularly important. Of the 1m females in the health service in 1970, for example, just over 40 per cent were part-time workers. Female labour, which was paid at lower rates than male workers, certainly appears to be an important reason why gross profits have been substantially higher than in manufacturing. In the mid 1960s, for example, the comparative averages were 33 and 21 per cent. By the mid 1970s, this had widened to the remarkable extent of 31 and 4 per cent, though unquestionably this partly reflected the heavy impact of world recession on manufacturing as well as problems of measurement.

It is by no means the whole story, however. As has been noted, services are far less easy prey to import penetration; and the broad financial sector fared well out of a sharp rise in inflation and the high interest rates which accompanied it in the early 1970s.

The geographical concentration of the relatively high *per capita* income services – especially in finance – in London and the South-East has for a long time been a feature of the British economy (Brown, 1972). It became even more pronounced during the period under consideration as the overall balance between manufacturing and services altered. Over the 1960s and 1970s costs of location and general expansion resulted in the growing importance of a belt extending from the South-East along either side of the M4 motorway to Bristol (Law, 1980). These developments contributed to a declared and growing sense of division between north and south, though it is impossible to say what have been its economic consequences. A series of measures to encourage office relocation in order to provide alternative employment opportunities and economic stimulus did something to modify the pattern though not fundamentally to change it. The record of the government itself in this respect was not impressive (ibid).

Whilst the relative decline of manufacturing was not a direct consequence of the expansion of services, there are obvious questions relating to the manner in which the relative attractiveness of services made it difficult for manufacturing to recruit high-quality labour and whether their geographical concentration reinforced metropolitan attitudes within central government administration and, thus, indirectly worked against a clear understanding of regional industrial decline. Even more problematical is the extent to which the higher costs generated in the South-East were passed on as external diseconomies to the rest of the economy: whether London was, and indeed continues to be, in Cobbett's phrase, 'this monstrous Wen . . . sucking up the vitals of the country'.

[1]   In theoretical terms, it cannot be assumed that it was disadvantageous for Britain to specialise in low productivity sectors, since it depends on what happens to relative prices between high and low productivity growth sectors. In other words, it depends on whether the high productivity sectors (or countries) were forced by competition to pass on their gains to customers in other countries through the terms of trade, that is through lower export prices. This outcome seems highly unlikely for this period when the broad pattern of comparative income and productivity growth between Britain and the other major economies is brought into consideration.

5
Corporate structure, management and labour

(i) Corporate structure

British manufacturing industry is highly concentrated. In 1970 the hundred largest firms accounted for 40 per cent of net output as compared with 25 per cent in the early 1950s. Alternative measures of concentration – such as capitalisation – give even higher ratios. For comparison, the figure for the USA in 1970 in terms of net output was just under 35 per cent (Hannah and Kay, 1977; Hart and Clarke, 1980). The 40 per cent level in the UK had already nearly been achieved by the early 1960s. It is noteworthy that the two slowest growing of the major economies since the Second World War – Britain and the USA – have also experienced the highest levels of concentration. Whether there is any causal relationship involved will be considered later. So far as other sectors are concerned there are no comparable data. Nevertheless, the pattern appears to have been broadly similar for finance, transport, oil refining and distribution. By contrast, in building and construction the small firm continued to dominate. Likewise, there were a range of services – including solicitors, garages, restaurants – where small scale remained the norm (Bolton Report, 1971). But by far the biggest service activity in terms of turnover is retailing. Here, there was a perceptible change. In 1950 multiples accounted for 22 per cent of total turnover, in 1966 for 33 per cent, and by 1971 for 37 per cent.

In many ways the most powerful impetus to greater concentrations came from the state. Within industry a unique area resulted from nationalisation. The actual form of organisation adopted was by no means standardised but in each case it was subject to direct political control (Chester, 1975). The government itself became larger and more concentrated in its operation as it assumed increasing responsibilities in areas such as education and defence. In turn this had a substantial impact on industrial organisation, most especially through the demand for labour and capital. One measure of this demand is that by the 1950s direct expenditure on goods and services by government was on average just over 20 per cent of GDP.

Statistical analysis has produced somewhat differing explanations of the causes of industrial concentration. For some the internal growth of firms is held to be the dominant force, with merger activity playing a distinctly secondary role (Prais, 1976; Hart and Clarke, 1980), whilst others hold that the opposite is the case (Hannah and Kay, 1977). There are two reasons why the latter is far more convincing. It conforms to the detailed historical evidence which is available and the occurrence of mergers in waves instead of as a continuous process undermines the statistical assumptions on which the former analysis is based. Indeed, in the 1960s there was a surge of merger activity which peaked over 1967/9. In total, mergers did not occur on quite the same scale as they did in the 1920s – which was equivalent to something like one-third of all firms in manufacturing going out of existence – but they caused the loss of an equivalent of a quarter of all firms.

Analysis has been limited to manufacturing, but similar trends were occurring in other sectors, and the process of concentration had features which are of more general significance. The most obvious of these was that mergers occurred in waves and affected all industries. It is a pattern which tells against analyses which present mergers largely as the outcome of marketing and technical factors which are specific to the industries concerned. Furthermore, detailed studies of company performance indicate that whatever the claims and expectations expressed before a merger they were not generally realised subsequently (Meeks, 1977). Similarly, in aggregate terms, the UK's high rate of concentration was not matched by a high rate of growth in manufacturing output. Such a lack of association could have been the outcome of a varying range of factors. For example, companies enjoying a strong monopolistic position may well have decided not to exploit it anywhere near fully and efficiently for fear of attracting undue public interest. The tobacco industry over the 1950s and 1960s is a good case in point. But the hard fact remains: in the UK increasing concentration in terms of corporate size was not matched by increases in plant size (Pratten, 1971; Cockerill and Silberston, 1974; Prais, 1981). What is more, plant size in the UK was significantly smaller than in the corresponding industries of its major competitors. All of which implies strongly that concentration in UK manufacturing industry was prompted by the rewards to be gained from ownership and control rather than from increased scale of production (Aaronvitch and Sawyer, 1975). Why was it so?

To begin with there was what might be termed the residual effect of the interwar years. At that time many amalgamations were the outcome of defensive alliances in the face of international competition and declining markets. As such, they were based on a loose holding-company structure which had not entailed thorough-going internal reorganisation. These forms persisted into the post-war years in such industries as cotton, iron and steel, shipbuilding and shipping. Even more modern industries such as motor vehicles, tobacco and electrical goods had adopted a similar pattern. In the sellers' markets of the post-war years there were no pressures for changing this *modus operandi* of business expansion.

The work of business historians is providing growing evidence that large size and a bigger market were in themselves major objectives in merger activity, which interestingly tends to confirm certain hypotheses of earlier theoretical literature (Cyert and March, 1963; Marris, 1964). Another aspect of these aims was the powerful attraction of establishing international companies for their own sake. In relation to its national income the UK has had a disproportionately very large number of companies among the largest 500 in the world (Prais, 1976). When comparative efficiency is taken into account, such a degree of concentration cannot be directly explained by Britain's reliance on international trade, though its traditional international role had obviously played an important part in conditioning business horizons. For all this, however, business cannot ignore minimum financial constraints without serious consequences, a fact which is certainly allowed for in most of the literature which nevertheless emphasises the non-profit maximising nature of merger activity. There are, however, reasons for doubting whether financial objectives were quite as secondary as these points suggest.

It has already been noted that, over the period, taxes on capital gains were either non-existent or very favourable as against taxes on profits and dividends (Kay and King, 1978). This differential amounted to a direct incentive to takeovers by means of share exchange or the use of undistributed profits, especially where the acquired company possessed capital assets which were under-valued in its balance sheet. In the 1950s, property assets were a major target and the boom in mergers was directly linked with the sharp upward movement in property prices. At the extreme, tax advantages gave rise to downright asset stripping. But, more generally, mergers represented the development of skills in the arts of corporate finance. Increasingly, these became allied to large firms which, apart from their main business, were becoming, by virtue of their size, mini capital markets. Comprehensive evaluation of company performance over these broader activities is not available, but the little which is known about individual companies suggests that financial objectives were more important than they might appear on the surface. Even so, a significant number of takeover bids were probably no more than a form of corporate conspicuous consumption.

The merger boom of the 1960s occurred within a general business ethos of 'big is beautiful'. The Labour government under Harold Wilson was especially vigorous in promoting the idea by word and deed (Blackaby, 1978). Convinced that Britain's out-dated industries could be drawn through 'the white heat of the technological revolution' only by means of amalgamation and rationalisation, in 1966 the government established an agency (the Industrial Reorganisation Corporation or IRC) and provided funds to bring it about. The policy was based on little more than a vague belief in the large potential for economies of scale and an unquenchable faith among politicians that government agencies could successfully meet short-term political demands – particularly in respect of regional unemployment – in combination with longer-term goals of greater efficiency and higher industrial growth. It also reflected a government preference for not pursuing a vigorous anti-monopoly policy or examining whether existing legislation in this sphere was operating successfully in relation to agreed criteria for business, and more general economic performance. An outstanding example was provided by the GEC merger with English Electric in 1968 in which its promoter, Arnold Weinstock, firmly believed he had been helped by government support through the IRC. The attitude of the government at the time was encapsulated by Anthony Crosland, president of the Board of Trade, when he stated (Jones and Marriott, 1970, *1*; cf. Bolton Report, 1971):

The government takes the view that the rationalization which the proposed merger would facilitate would increase the efficiency and productivity of the electrical engineering industries, and in particular the effectiveness of the export effort of the companies whose overseas sales are of the greatest importance to the Balance of Payments.

(ii) Management

Changes in the scale of business organisation were not matched by the adoption of modern methods of organisation and management, even though such claims were usually at the centre of the public case for a merger (Channon, 1973; Meeks, 1977). Although British industry more than matched American in its degree of concentration it was far slower to adopt modern methods of business organisation, especially the multi-divisional company form which had been well established in the USA before the Second World War. With a few exceptions, it was not until the 1960s that large companies in Britain began to close the gap. In a number of cases, though probably not the majority, the public or 'outsider' case for a merger was devised to conceal – or certainly not to reveal – the 'insider' objectives behind a merger proposal, which were far more concerned with private financial gain than the company reorganisation (Aaronvitch and Sawyer, 1975). Over and above this, however, company promotion involved a different set of entrepreneurial skills from company development, a fact brought out most vividly in those cases where merger or takeover operations failed. An interesting example – both in terms of scale and impact – was the takeover bid for Courtaulds made by ICI in 1962 (Coleman, 1980). Heralded by the press as the biggest takeover in British history, it was a complex manoeuvre of commercial aggrandisement by ICI. It failed because it precipitated a managerial revolution in Courtaulds, which in turn led to the defeat of the bid and the rapid recovery of the company. This was not a common experience, however; indeed, shortly afterwards Courtaulds itself embarked on the takeover trail.

Deficiencies in company organisation were persistent. Inadequate cost-accounting practices, poor marketing, bad industrial relations, slow rates of technical innovation: all these were revealed as major weaknesses in comparisons drawn between Britain and her major competitors (Pagnamenta and Overy, 1984). Management training thus became a particular focus of attention. Two business schools were established – at London and Manchester – in the 1960s. In comparison with Britain's major competitors this amounted to pathetically little [Hannah, 1983]. And more trained managers did not directly result in operational changes in business organisation. In part this was because of the scale of the problems involved, particularly in such industries as shipbuilding, motor cars and aircraft (Bhaskar, 1979). More generally, there was a growing belief over the 1960s and into the 1970s that Britain's industrial problems could be overcome through more vigorous entrepreneurship, the supply of which was held to be 'market-determined'. Hence the government had a major role to play not simply through the provision of business training but by means of supplying financial incentives through the taxation system. Such an approach ignored the complexity of modern business organisation as well as the evidence on taxation levels from abroad (Phelps Brown, 1977). Moreover, it did little to alter the relative financial attractiveness of occupations.

Entrepreneurial strategies – as distinct from their managerial implementation – centre on investment, marketing and the form of company organisation. But although they can be fairly clearly defined they are the outcome of complex relationships within the firm such that entrepreneurship is diffused through different levels of management, frequently to a degree that the operative distinction between entrepreneur and manager no longer applies (Alford, 1976). In so far as top businessmen play a decisive role in company strategy – as distinct from its public presentation – the talents they need will vary from one situation to another. The kind of entrepreneur required in a new and expanding industry is likely to be somewhat different from the one required to handle the contraction and reorganisation of an old staple industry. 'Horses for courses' in this context implies that entrepreneurial (and managerial) mobility is at least as important as its initial recruitment. Not surprisingly, therefore, entrepreneurs and managers can become locked into an existing company structure which may perform not particularly well but adequately enough to survive, or to survive while its position is steadily being undermined by import penetration.

There are strong grounds for arguing that these conditions were particularly acute in British industry. The inheritance of outmoded company structures from the past, reinforced by further concentration, produced very rigid company organisation. Until the early 1960s external pressures were not, in the main, strong enough to precipitate crises within companies, forcing them into radical reorganisation. Companies survived even though their markets and profit margins were narrowing. Indeed, in an absolute sense a large part of British business was not suffering from a lack of market opportunities – as growing import penetration bears ample witness – but its capacity to exploit them was steadily weakening. As with so many things in the real economic world, these processes were not smoothly reversible once they were perceived, and they became rapidly critical in the mid 1960s when companies in a wide range of industries ran into severe problems. The crisis occurred not just in the old industries such as steel and shipbuilding but in artificial fibres, electrical goods and, *par excellence*, motor manufacture.

Masterplans of one sort or another were devised for ailing firms and even for whole industries (Blackaby, 1978; Morris, 1979). More often than not these involved cooperation with the government as the only available paymaster. Parallel to this there were demands for the encouragement of small firms (Bolton Report, 1971). In certain cases individual businessmen had considerable success in setting companies on more prosperous paths. But even these demonstrated that the dynamics of change were largely generated by outside pressures and not by self-starting entrepreneurship. There were areas in which the more traditional, buccaneering type of entrepreneur still played a role. Retailing, electronics, printing and publishing, and commodity trading, provide major examples. Whatever their immediate contribution to business enterprise and development, nevertheless the transition of their companies into successful national and even international companies depended on their early adoption of modern forms of company organisation and management. The much publicised financial successes which exclusive ownership generally brought to these individuals when they 'went public' easily obscures this fact.

Major shortcomings in company organisation and management have been at the centre of Britain's unsatisfactory economic performance. There is, however, the more fundamental issue of whether these shortcomings emanate from deeper social attitudes which view manufacturing industry as an inferior form of human activity. Over recent years the literature on this has focused on the late Victorian period as the source of the problem (Coleman, 1973; Wiener, 1981). It has presented a picture of a large number of upper-middle-class families drawing their substantial incomes from industry whilst moving in a *milieu* which extolled and practised the alleged virtues of the English gentleman. Somewhat improbably this creature of advanced civilisation was produced by means of a liberal education in the semi-barbarous institution of the English public school. The dichotomy between these elements was resolved by turning the boardroom into a form of club to which only those with the right social background would be admitted. In some ways this was but a different form of much older attitudes towards 'trade'. What was new was the scale of its economic implications and its worship of the cult of the amateur who led and of the practical man who did. For both, professionalism was anathema. In certain occupations, particularly in engineering, there were changes which improved standards of training and established professional status through the formation of recognised institutions. The problem was that these developments were largely and necessarily outside the university system. Over the longer run this had the effect of bestowing an inferior status on these professions in comparison with those, such as lawyers and doctors, which had standing in the established seats of learning.

The attitudes set in late Victorian times can be traced in British industry right through into our period. Perhaps most striking, has been their persistence even in the new science-based industries of the twentieth century (Pagnamenta and Overy, 1984). It is not possible, of course, to be certain of the extent of their deleterious effect without a great deal more investigation. But there is already much evidence to support the presumption that the effect was pervasive. The contrasts which can be drawn with foreign industry – even with such a tradition-bound country as France – are often stark. The widening of educational opportunity in the immediate post-war period was not accompanied by radical changes in its content. Despite successive attempts, there was a failure to establish vocational education on a par with more traditional forms (Robbins, 1963). Hence, the careers open to the talents were being sought, as much as ever, in the professions, the civil service or finance and not in manufacturing industry. Over the 1960s wearers of the old school tie probably became less evident in the boardroom and the higher reaches of management, but were not generally replaced by an elite drawn from the new cadres of higher education. Perhaps the greatest deficiencies in the relationship between education and industry occurred in the training and recruitment of middle management. Business histories provide much evidence of weakness at this level.

The problem, however, lies in distinguishing cause and effect. A mere listing of impressionistic and selective evidence of anti-business attitudes does not advance understanding very far (Wiener, 1981). Over the period, spokesmen for industry identified government and the major educational institutions as the villains; and the business and professional careers of many leading politicians lend credence by example to such charges. Yet it is equally possible to see the faults lying with industry in its failure to provide opportunities attractive enough to overcome the alleged prejudice against it. More investigation may well reveal that manufacturing industry simply did not pay enough to get the best people. Certainly, time and again the evidence suggests rigidity of attitudes and practices as industry's most apparent characteristics. There is no reason why management should be an exception to the rule: bad frequently breeds worse.

(iii) Labour

In popular terms more responsibility for Britain's lack of international competitiveness has been laid at the door of trade unions than at that of management; an attitude strongly encouraged by the high political profile which unions have adopted since 1945. More sober assessments may well modify this view, but the nature of trade unionism and its part in industrial relations remains central to the analysis. By its nature, this area – in common with management performance – is not one which can be analysed by the Cartesian methods of economists. Economists are nothing if not ingenious, however, and in their ingenuity they have done much to deflect attention away from searching investigation into the nature and operation of organised labour within individual firms and industries. The most celebrated attempt to explain it all by numbers was the so-called Phillips curve (1958). Simply stated, it claimed – on the basis of long-run data on wages and unemployment – that there was a trade-off between the level of unemployment and the rate of change of wages; and that union bargaining and other influences – such as changes in the structure of the labour market – were of secondary importance in the process of determining the level of wages and, presumably, wage-costs. Subsequently, variations on this theme were advanced (Purdy and Zis, 1974). There have been numerous and convincing criticisms of the data used in these exercises and of their disregard of other forces, in particular of the causal influence of prices on wage demands and of complex institutional pressures which result in marked stickiness in downward adjustments of wage rates (Phelps Brown, 1975). Nevertheless the Phillips curve had a siren appeal in the later 1950s and early 1960s because of the ease with which it could be translated into part of aggregate demand management. Hence in 1964 Paish, an influential economist, based policy recommendations on it, in particular the need to maintain a margin of unemployment to keep wage demands in check (Blackaby, 1978; Paish, 1962, 1968). When in the late 1960s wages and unemployment began to move together and then to accelerate rapidly the Phillips curve became somewhat discredited, despite various theoretical attempts made to rescue it. Yet by the mid 1970s policy-makers, convinced that we live in a world of free markets, began to display an implied belief in its basic tenets (Brittan, 1975; Harris and Sewill, 1975). By the early 1980s it had become a matter of faith.

Recently, there has been notable self-criticism among senior economists for not having given much more attention to the problem of income determination within the framework of Keynesian analysis (Meade, 1982). However, it is questionable whether this recantation at the level of economic theory provides the clue as to the practical reasons why the road to the high inflation of the 1970s was littered with the wrecks of attempts at incomes policies. Between 1955 and 1965 average wage rates rose by 4 per cent, from then until 1974 9 per cent, and in 1975 by 30 per cent (Prest and Coppock). The machinery of incomes policies which was invented ranged from the primitive level of Selwyn Lloyd's pay pause (1961) and 'guiding light' (a 4 per cent norm) to the bureaucratic sophistication of the Prices and Incomes Board (1965). Finally, government and unions entered into a Faustian agreement known as the 'social contract' (1974), in which the government proved to be well and truly cast in the principal role.

Trade union development was one of slow growth in membership until the mid 1960s followed by much faster recruitment until, by the early 1970s, over half the workforce was unionised (Clegg, 1972). The expansion of white-collar unionism was a particular feature of the most recent phase. Parallel to what was happening in the company sector, mergers increased union concentration (Hannah and Kay, 1977). Similarly there is little indication of concentration leading to major 'managerial' restructuring of union organisation or to change in traditional attitudes. Partly as a consequence of incomes policy and more directly as a result of efforts at reform, the government became increasingly involved in trade unions. A major official enquiry in 1968 – the Donovan Commission – was followed by a new grand strategy with an equally grand name: *In Place of Strife* (1969). The unions would not accept it and the Labour government thus abandoned it. Declarations of intent remained the order of the day.

The theoretical literature on industrial relations is mainly based on the national developments just outlined. There is some reason for such an approach since agreements between management and labour were reached within a framework of national collective bargaining. To the charge that the enormous number of local agreements can be cited as evidence of national agreements acting as little more than guidelines, the answer is given that local agreements acted as a form of pace-setting for subsequent national agreements, and that this transfer mechanism can be incorporated into wage-determination models (Prest and Coppock, 1978). The existence of this mechanism has yet to be convincingly demonstrated, however (Brown, 1981). More pointedly, such analyses are concerned with measuring the effects of wage movements; the causes have to be sought in the actual, real-world process of industrial relations – an environment as uncongenial to economists as it has been to many industrial managers.

A number of studies have brought out the bargaining strength of trade unions during the period of near full employment (Brown, 1981), which enabled them to reinforce long-established work practices which were an incubus on British industry in the form of overmanning. For much of the period overmanning was absorbed at the cost of lower absolute levels of productivity (despite the quite good record in terms of productivity growth), and the full extent of the burden was not revealed until the late 1970s as international competition drove sectors of British industry to the point of collapse (Prais, 1981). For the period under discussion, therefore, there is a central question of the extent to which high employment was purchased at the price of low productivity. Impressive though productivity growth was by Britain's historical standards, the absolute level of productivity was well below what was required for international competitiveness (Pratten, 1976b).

A leading writer on industrial relations has identified the mid 1960s as a kind of 'hinge' in the system of wage bargaining (Phelps Brown, 1975). The idea is that there was a swing in attitudes among rank and file unionists away from an acceptance of a number of necessary constraints on wage increases – an attitude strongly influenced by pre-war experience of high unemployment and post-war economic control – to rising expectations of wage increases as part and parcel of the much vaunted ethos of high and sustainable economic growth. The demonstration effect of rising real wages in Europe was another powerful stimulus to these expectations. Bound up with this change, and giving further impetus to it, was a shift in the centre of bargaining from national to local level – to the 'militancy and *dynamisme de la base*' (Phelps Brown, 1975, 5) which had not suffered the searing experience of mass unemployment. But these major changes in expectations and actions took place within the existing system of industrial relations and work practices. Hence a sharp 'hinge' movement instead of a break with the past. So long as full employment was sustained by government policy, wage inflation was a natural consequence.

More emphasis should be placed on this conjuncture of forces than on the strike record. In international comparisons of working days lost Britain does not show up as particularly strike prone (Smith, 1980). But the figures tell only part of the story. In the USA, for example, a large number of days may be lost in an industry while new productivity deals are being negotiated; the immediate loss of production is just part of the price paid for high levels of output over the longer run. By contrast, in Britain the pattern has been one of small disruptive strikes – often over job demarcation or manning levels – which have had serious long-term effects on output quality, delivery dates and labour costs, leading to a corrosive loss of markets both at home and abroad (Phelps Brown, 1977). Productivity measures mask these things because of the ratchet-like effect of loss of market share.

Trade unions have been far more suspicious of serious histor-ical enquiry than their business counterparts, and investigations into particular disputes have tended to be within pre-determined sets of assumptions about the relationship between so-called labour and capital (Beynon, 1984). Similarly, much recent ana-lysis of the impact of technical change on labour relations has been concerned to show how technical innovation has been driven by the need of employers to 'deskill' the workforce in order to control the 'work process' and extract the maximum rate of profits from labour (Friedman, 1977). Quite apart from the problem of reconciling these propositions with internationally comparative evidence on rises in real wages, increases in the share of wages in national income, and the growth of the service sector, the analysis fails to take account of the skills created by new technology – skills which have been exploited to powerful effect by those who possess and control them. More careful and critical studies reveal the all too well-known pattern of the failure of British workers to employ new techniques as effectively as their foreign counterparts, to both their own and the general loss (Dore, 1973; Pratten, 1976b).

In some ways employers effectively connived with the unions in sustaining costly work practices. There were industries in which managers had for years sub-contracted certain management tasks to labour – for example the gang-work systems in steel, dockyards and shipbuilding – and similar practices operated in such industries as motorcar and aircraft production. More generally, over the 1950s and early 1960s many employers 'hoarded' labour in the expectation of government sustaining a buoyant level of domestic demand. Hence, if increased trade union bargaining power led to high wage settlements they could be passed on to the consumer in the form of higher prices.

A series of influences tended to reduce the labour cost-consciousness of management, particularly in manufacturing industries. To begin with, there was the accumulated pre-war experience, which stretched back into the nineteenth century, of labour being the cheap factor of production – an attitude reflected in the slow development of cost-accounting in Britain. During the Second World War the whole economic effort centred on supplying and employing sufficient quantities of labour and materials. Costs were secondary. These fundamental needs persisted into the post-war period. Recovery occurred within a market in which everything which was produced could be sold. The main marketing problem was rationing not price competitiveness. For some sectors of industry this remained the situation until as late as 1955. When, finally, remaining wartime controls were abolished these influences did not suddenly disappear. Markets were buoyant and the maintenance of a high level of demand was thought to be the key to sustained prosperity. Competitiveness did not readily become part of the common parlance of British industry.

In sum, it is argued that whilst much more research needs to be done in the field of business organisation, management and labour, sufficient evidence already exists to identify these as key areas in the explanation of Britain's comparatively poor economic performance.

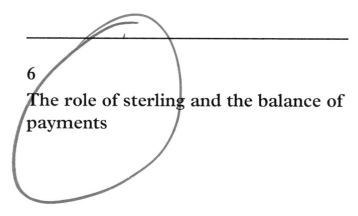

6
The role of sterling and the balance of payments

There is much debate as to whether there was a Keynesian revolution in domestic economic policy in the post-war period (Peden, 1987). The more interesting question is whether Keynes's greater influence was over Britain's international financial policy through his dominant role in the negotiations which led to the Bretton Woods agreement of 1944 and to the American loan of 1945. These two arrangements, which directly and indirectly committed Britain to major international financial responsibilities in which the operation of sterling as a reserve currency was an essential element, stemmed from a deeper commitment to the belief in Britain's world role (Clarke, 1982; Scammell, 1980; Strange, 1971). In fairness to Keynes, he had argued for a much wider, multilateral system than was in fact agreed, though even this involved the assumption that Britain would not face a dollar problem after the immediate post-war financial adjustment (Keynes, 1946).

In sharp contrast there has been an attempt to argue that Britain's adherence to the sterling area was not determined by an anachronistic desire to play a world role, combined with a suspicious prejudice against integration with Europe, but was the result of a careful balancing of post-war economic needs (Newton, 1984). It involved support for international economic expansion promoted by the USA and for agreements between European governments in reviving trade, particularly with countries of the Eastern hemisphere. Britain's leadership of the sterling area is thus seen as a crucial link in this scheme of things. Marshall Aid (1948) is cast as the villain since its concentration on Western European problems did not solve the wider dollar problem and, hence, intensified disequilibrium in world trade. Only America's continuing desire for political and military hegemony – which erupted into the Korean war – saved the day by causing an increasing outflow of dollars. Such an argument would appear, however, to overestimate vastly the potential contribution of the 'Eastern hemisphere' in the post-war process of adjustment while ignoring the strength of European economic recovery which depended so much on intraregional trade in manufactured goods. For Europe, Marshall Aid was an important element in its recovery: for Britain it was first a safeguard and then a prop to the sterling area (cf. Milward, 1984).

In passing judgement on these crucial issues the historian is so easily blinkered by hindsight. He has to ask: was there any real alternative? At the time, certainly alternative courses were being urged. Most importantly, the Americans were keen to see the sterling balances settled on an economically sound basis (Van Dormael, 1978; Strange, 1971). Moreover, if the USA was suspicious of perfidious Albion, it was increasingly fearful of the spread of communism and convinced of the need for an economically and democratically strong Western Europe as a bulwark against it (Louis, 1977). As has been suggested earlier, the opportunity was open to Britain to bargain with the US for some reduction in her international responsibilities during the negotiations over the American loan in 1945. As late as 1947 the opportunity was apparently still available. With American fears of communist advance at their height and the sterling/dollar exchange crisis raging, opportunity and need had never been greater. There was, in fact, no desire amongst policy-makers for change (Conan, 1961). The government, especially in the person of the Foreign Secretary, Ernest Bevin, feared communism in Europe as much as the Americans: the difference was that for him it meant keeping Europe firmly at arm's length (Bullock, 1983). Outside the political arena powerful support for the policy came from two sources: the City and the Treasury (Day, 1954; Radcliffe, 1959). For the former the sterling area was good for business; for the latter, an international financial role for Britain involved direct responsibilities which placed it in the central position in government to which it had become accustomed before 1939 but had lost over the war years. In sum, alternative policies for sterling were not carefully considered at that time, not because they were unrealistic but because they were politically uncongenial and ran counter to powerful vested interests (Bauer and Walters, 1975).

The convertibility crisis of 1947 was met with the 'export drive'. It was very successful. More successful, indeed, than even contemporaries realised because of inaccuracies in the official statistics which were available. As had been noted, however, growth in the world market was a more important cause of the success than improvement in British competitive performance. Moreover, the major source of under-recording on the balance of payments up to 1949 was invisible trade. The fundamental difficulty, nevertheless, was that contemporaries had not 'foreseen ... that the balance of payments on current account and the change in the gold and dollar reserves would bear little relationship to one another' (Cairncross, 1985, 79); in particular there was a heavy outflow of capital to the sterling area. In 1949 another financial crisis occurred which led to the massive devaluation of the pound against the dollar from $4.00 to $2.80 (Cairncross and Eichengreen, 1983). If attention is directed simply at annual balance of payments figures the decision appears surprising since 1949 was a year of further *overall* improvement. *Within* the year, however, there were very sharp movements resulting from the self-reinforcing effects of a mild depression in the USA, short-term stock piling adjustments in the UK which resulted in high imports, speculative expectations of devaluation and short-term measures to safeguard reserves. The official response was equally conditioned by short-term considerations centring on the reserve position and by lack of understanding of the issues involved.

The basic problem, as recent analysis has shown, was one of long-term adjustment of the dollar in relation to the pound and other major currencies. From the UK's viewpoint, the time was right in 1949 as by then it had the productive capacity to take advantage of the added price competitiveness in dollar markets which devaluation would provide, while needing to rely less heavily on imports from those areas. Because this advantage was not understood, the devaluation was made too late and was not effectively exploited. The subsequent improvement in the balance of payments clearly owed something to devaluation but its effect is impossible to disentangle because of the general improvement in world markets. In mitigation of these charges it has sometimes been claimed that 'an important by-product of devaluation was an improvement in USA–UK economic relations' (Cairncross, 1985, *142*). But was this a good thing? It can just as easily be seen as Britain accepting subservience under the US in preference to engaging in fuller European economic cooperation.

It may seem unduly harsh or unfair to criticise the achievements of the export drive. Unlike the issue of sterling there would seem to have been little choice in the line of action to be followed. Yet it cannot alter the fact that short-term success had costly long-term effects. Whilst exports to the dollar area rose by three times in current terms between 1947 and 1951, as a share of total exports the increase (from 11.5 to 14.5 per cent) was only marginal. In 1948 exports to the hard currency countries (which, in order of size, were South Africa, Canada, the USA, Argentina, Sweden, Belgium, Switzerland) were 25 per cent of the total. Detailed analysis of the remaining 75 per cent is not possible here but official statistics show that it relied heavily on soft markets desperate for basic manufactured goods. Textiles alone accounted for nearly one-quarter of the total. Moreover, to switch exports from soft sterling markets to hard currency countries would have been largely self-defeating because the former would then seek imports from hard currency areas thus causing a balancing drain on reserves.

Consideration of marketing and all it implied in terms of design, reliability, delivery and servicing, was of little importance against the basic problem of production for a world market in which there was a substantial margin of unsatisfied demands. When, for example, the suspension of British motor cars collapsed under continental road conditions or when spare parts were not available for machine tools, initially only the reputation of British goods was damaged; but the frequency of such occurrences amounted to a large accumulation of market ill-will by the early 1950s (Pagnamenta and Overy, 1984). By contrast, countries such as France, Germany and Japan entered world markets later and needed to fight their way back into them under conditions of growing competition. Their methods differed accordingly (Shonfield, 1965).

Britain's declining share of world trade is clearly indicated in Table II above. The level of the early 1950s was abnormal in the sense that major trading nations were still recovering from internal war devastation. Over the subsequent period, however, the falling share was substantially more than would be expected simply as a result of peace-time adjustments – probably to the extent of between 20 and 30 per cent (Fetherston *et al.*, 1977). Germany and Japan, in particular, gained at the expense of the UK. The fall in export share was in substantial part explained by a fall in the UK share of world output of manufactured goods. Significantly, however, the export share fell even more sharply, especially over the 1950s and 1960s (Batchelor *et al.*, 1980). Within this the commodity composition showed a marked increase in engineering products which rose from 37 per cent in 1955 to 45 per cent in 1970 of total UK exports; semi-manufactures (including chemicals, textiles and metals) fell from 30 per cent to 26 per cent because of the decline in textiles, while other manufactures remained fairly constant around 13 per cent and non-manufactures fell from 25 per cent to 15 per cent. In terms of area the share of Western Europe rose from 29 to nearly 50 per cent, North America from 12 to 16 per cent, while the sterling area (developed) fell from 23 to 13 per cent and the sterling area (developing) from 22 to 12 per cent. Overall the share of UK exports going to the developed world rose from 66 to 77 per cent. The picture is completed by the figures for import penetration. What is then vividly revealed is that British industry's inability to match the pace of competition in foreign markets forced it to rely proportionately more on the home market but, in turn, it failed to hold its position. This led to the 'market tapering' to which reference has already been made (Chapter 3). Although these weaknesses did not show up in the balance of payments until the 1960s this does not mean that the position in the 1950s was anywhere near 'entirely satisfactory' since the process was then in the making (cf. Tomlinson, 1985).

Britain's loss of overseas markets has been explained largely in terms of the qualitative factors such as design and poor delivery, to which reference has been made (Caves, 1968; Stout, 1976). The evidence is compelling. At the same time, the element of price competitiveness must not be forgotten. A decision by a customer to change a source of supply usually involves substantial fixed costs in setting up new systems of distribution and servicing which cannot be immediately written off against lower supply prices. However, once the market for a good had been lost because, in combination with other factors, the price was too high, the position could not be recovered easily simply by lowering the price. Britain's lack of competitiveness in the 1960s was clearly the product of some combination of comparative productive inefficiency and the rate of exchange (Thirlwall, 1982). The devaluation of 1967 (which reduced the dollar rate of the £ from $2.80 to $2.40) did something to redress the balance for perhaps two or three years but, for the reasons discussed earlier, its impact was limited (Artus, 1975).

Sterling was probably overvalued for most of the period from 1950 to 1967, especially against the European and Japanese currencies (Allsopp, 1979). Even so, the potential gain from a lower rate – even if it had been negotiable through the International Monetary Fund – is not easy to estimate because of the problems of relative elasticities of demand for both exports and imports and the problem of the cost effects of higher import prices, not least as they would have affected wage bargaining (Ball, 1967). On all the evidence it is highly improbable that overvaluation was the dominant constraint; particularly since import penetration occurred in a ratchet-like fashion. Whatever the exchange rate, foreign suppliers were benefiting from a lack of domestic manufacturing capacity, a deficiency which was a direct result of Britain's comparatively low level of productivity.

For similar reasons, not much weight can be given to the argument that balance of payments difficulties arose from persistent excess absorption (i.e. too high a level of demand) in the economy (Matthews *et al.*, 1982). In one sense the argument is tautological, since if less were consumed at home more would be available for export. In terms of international comparison, however, demand pressure was not unduly high in Britain. What does stand out is the way in which absorption patterns were changing as real incomes rose and the inability of domestic industry to match these patterns in terms of resource use and productivity.

Table XIII *UK trade and payments 1946–75*

	Visible trade balance	Invisible trade balance	Current balance	Investment and other capital transactions	Total official financing	Balancing item
1946	−103	−127	−230	+235[a]	−54	50[a]
1947	−361	−20	−381	+342[a]	+210	−150[a]
1948	−151	+177	+26	−128[a]	+70	−100[a]
1949	−137	+136	−1	−106[a]	+3	−50[a]
1950	−51	+358	+307	+128[a]	−575	—[a]
1951	−689	+320	369	+92[a]	+334	+100[a]
1952	−279	+442	+163	−404	+175	+66
1953	−244	+389	+145	+119	−296	+32
1954	−204	+321	+117	−48	−126	+57
1955	−313	+158	−155	−195	+229	+121
1956	+53	+155	+208	−409	+159	+42
1957	−29	+262	+233	−300	−13	+80
1958	+29	+331	+360	−121	−290	+51
1959[b]	−115	+287	+172	−108	+40	−46
1960[b]	−401	+173	−228	+286	−293	+267
1961	−140	+187	+47	−316	+339	−70
1962	−100	+255	+155	−3	−192	+40
1963	−119	+244	+125	−100	+58	−83
1964	−543	+185	−358	−311	+695	−26
1965	−260	+230	−30	−317	+353	−6
1966[b]	−108	+238	+130	−580	+591	−97
1967[b]	−599	+330	−269	−504	+671	+207
1968[b]	−712	+468	−244	−760	+1,410	−155
1969	−209	+714	+505	−176	−687	+358
1970[b]	−34	+857	+823	+546	−1,420	−82
1971[b]	+190	+934	+1,124	+1,790	−3,271	+232
1972[b]	−748	+995	+247	−684	+1,141	−828
1973	−2,586	+1,605	−981	+166	+771	+103
1974	−5,351	+2,078	−3,273	+1,594	+1,646	+108
1975	−3,333	+1,812	−1,521	+137	+1,465	−81

Source: Economic Trends Annual Supplement 1983. [a] Estimates. [b] Figures for these years do not strictly balance because of special financial transactions.

The broad features of the balance of payments are shown in Table XIII. The crisis years of 1955, 1964, 1967 and 1974 stand out when individual accounts are examined, but since these are end-of-year figures and therefore include the effects of corrective measures, the full extent of payments difficulties is not revealed. Indeed, throughout the 1960s successive governments were struggling to balance the books and it was rather a case of some years being less bad than others. What is particularly interesting from the historical viewpoint is the manner in which refinement of the statistical data has altered the record. The most up-to-date figures present a less black picture than was thought to be the case at the time. A classic example of this is 1964 when at one stage the current deficit was reckoned to be £800m whereas the most recent figure puts the actual deficit for that year at £355m (Blackaby, 1978). Refinement is perhaps something of a euphemism since these alterations resulted from differing estimates of the degree of error in the data, and frequently the figures show a large balancing item which is the sum total of errors and omissions. Accordingly, sophisticated econometric analyses of balance of payments behaviour should be treated with strong scepticism. The really intriguing historical problems, which await further investigation, concern the manner in which policy-makers reacted to this inaccurate information in determining policy and the way in which it affected external relations, especially with international financial institutions, in particular the International Monetary Fund.

Britain's weak balance of payments was not, however, a statistical delusion or the result of a reaction to one. If less bad than was thought, it was still bad. The economy's heavy reliance on trade, combined with government responsibility for maintaining the value of sterling, made the balance of payments a central issue of the political economy of the period (Beckerman, 1972; Dornbusch and Fisher, 1980). In the early 1960s a number of economists went so far as to argue that growth had to be export-led (Kaldor, 1971). Evidence was cited from other economies to reveal a high correlation between the two. But correlation is not causation. Consequently, prescriptive analysis was ambiguous: sustained export demand, not subject to stop/go, was seen as the driving force yet dependent on improved competitiveness; whether this improvement was itself dependent on export demand was never clearly specified. Frequent references to German and Japanese experience failed to recognise that their export drives (based on new goods, new markets and new marketing techniques) had been made in the 1950s and their very success changed the trading world as well as their own economies. Britain was too late an arrival at the feast. Similarly the effectiveness of export-led growth in the British case cannot be squared with the continued rise of import penetration and the level of domestic demand which this represented.

Invisibles were the bright spot in the balance of payments. But, as has been shown, although their proportionate contribution increased over the period it is not something which should be interpreted in wholly optimistic terms. At the time, moreover, there were those who were prepared to challenge the glowing claims by spokesmen for city institutions before the Radcliffe enquiry (Day, 1954; Radcliffe, 1959; Shonfield, 1959). Over the 1960s the issue became more stark as the underlying position of visible trade worsened. Balance of payments crises were registered through the balance of short-term assets and liabilities; and a number of critics, then as now, fastened on the level of overseas military expenditure which in international terms was disproportionately high in relation to national income. But should such expenditure be counted as a loss any more than additional imports? In this respect the issue was primarily a question of what could be afforded. It was not a cause of poor economic performance; it was yet another consequence of the attitudes which were shaping that performance.

Throughout the period under examination Britain had a negative balance on the flow of long-term overseas investment. Correspondingly this affected the basic balance, i.e. the current balance plus the balance of long-term capital flow. Under the system of fixed exchange rates any export of capital affected the reserve position though precisely how depended on the manner in which the investment was financed. From the mid 1960s to the early 1970s the finance of direct investment through foreign borrowing and overseas profits in fact resulted in a small net balance to be added to the reserves. The existence of controls on investment in the non-sterling area therefore probably had little restrictive effect (Blackaby, 1978; Tew, 1982). Regulation of portfolio investment would appear to have been much more effective in the light of the surge in it following the removal of restrictions in 1979. Until the float of sterling in 1972 there were no strong restrictions on investment within the sterling area.

These facts by no means dispose of the controversy over the effects on economic performance of overseas investment. In whatever way it is financed, such investment is regarded by some as having been a direct loss to the domestic economy and as such having contributed to Britain's poor investment record (Singh, 1977). For a number of reasons, such analyses are simplistic. There are good grounds for thinking that to a significant degree home and foreign capital markets were separate and gave rise to quite different levels of investment expectations. A complete block on foreign investment might well have resulted in less investment overall; and the fact that so much was financed by overseas borrowing is of particular significance here. Quite simply, the alternative of more home investment was not attractive. In other respects, foreign investment may be essential for the domestic economy. It may finance demands for exports either directly or indirectly. Substantial investments in distribution systems or overseas plants may be the only means of overcoming barriers which otherwise would make it impossible to reap the full returns from a given technical process. The use of particular skills in mining or property development may well yield good returns from abroad. In practice, investment does not divide easily into outflows and inflows – complex inter-relationships exist between the two and, further, they are part of a multilateral system of capital movement. Added to this, capital flows are important vectors of technical change. Over the 1950s, for example, large amounts of US capital were invested in Britain because of the wide productivity gap which existed between the economies. A policy of investment autarky could well have been very costly in terms of lost economic growth (Dunning, 1979; Gomulka, 1979; Reddaway *et al.*, 1967, 1968).

Precise evaluation of the effects of overseas investment nevertheless remains extremely difficult. The only major attempt dealt with the period between the mid 1950s and the mid 1960s (Reddaway, 1967, 1968). Even then it was found impossible to make more than rough estimates of overseas investment despite regulations concerning disclosure and the remittance of profits. Devices such as internal pricing made it relatively easy for international companies to disguise the transmission of funds in or out of the country, quite apart from the purely technical problem of valuing overseas assets. For what it is worth, the general conclusion which emerged was that overseas investment had a small positive effect on exports. The wider effects, as has been observed, were not measurable, though the export advantages were probably reduced to the extent that investment went to highly developed economies. More recently, the Wilson Committee (1980), while unable to offer any firm conclusions, was at pains to question the value of overseas investment. It did so by drawing attention to the comparatively high percentage of gross domestic product invested abroad (1.4% on average over 1968 to 1978 as compared with 0.7% for the USA, 0.6% for Sweden, 0.5% for West Germany and 0.3% for Japan and France) and to the increasing proportion of this amount going to advanced economies, particularly to Western Europe. But the committee's calculations, by assuming cause and effect, made no allowances for absolute differences in *per capita* income or the proportionate level of exports in GDP. The committee's general ambivalence probably reflected its membership though it did admit that recent investigations suggested that to some extent investment was going abroad because of the unfavourable economic environment at home. Notwithstanding the need for more investigation, the evidence surveyed in the previous chapter certainly lends weight to this view.

Restrictions on external dealings have been a recurrent prescription for the cure of British economic ills. Tariffs have been particularly favoured. There are well-known objections to tariffs imposed to protect ailing industries and these are fully recognised by the most up-to-date protectionists who regard such tariffs as a primitive form which they call creeping protectionism (Cripps and Godley, 1978; Godley, 1979; Singh, 1977). Instead, they have argued for non-discriminatory tariffs which, in effect, would be imposed in a way which would take the existing level of imports as a baseline. To achieve this, sufficient domestic tax relief would be given to compensate for higher import prices resulting from tariffs up to current levels of imports. In addition there would be some further tax relief to stimulate growth which could then be supplied through home production. In this way, it is argued, the foreigner would not lose and the British economy would gain through growth. The restriction of world trade and output, inflation, feather-bedding of inefficiency, retaliation: all these standard objections would allegedly be taken care of by the proposed system. But even if the analysis is internally consistent, as a prescriptive policy it appears intellectually naïve in the light of historical evidence, especially that for the period between the wars. What is assumed is an unreal world in which governments would be able to resist the pressures and demands of this union or that business corporation for tariff adjustments to meet particular vested interests. When the theoretical assumptions themselves are examined the case is even less convincing.

The adjustment mechanisms are assumed to operate smoothly as the new opportunities are grasped. In the light of industry's past performance such adjustment does not seem likely. The argument begs the massive question of why productivity has been absolutely so low for so long. Production might well rise but would it not most probably be high-cost? Certain firms might go to the wall under domestic competition but, as the proponents of the policy admit, 'the British economy *as a whole* is being feather-bedded' (Godley, 1979, *233*). Unless it is prodded and pulled by the government, what is to stop it rolling over into a more comfortable position? And this brings the argument full circle to the question of government competence.

Another major problem turns on the assumptions relating to competitiveness. Enough evidence is available to show how, in the success of foreign imports and the failure of British exports, price was only one factor (Chapter 3). In other words, over some differential range of prices for imports and domestically produced substitutes there was a low cross-price elasticity of demand. The question then arises: how high would the tariff have to be to alter the relationship? Proponents of protection talk in terms of 'high' tariffs. Automatically this implies substantial tax reductions. What would be the redistributive effects of such cuts? How would they be financed? What, in turn, and given differing elasticities, would be the effects on inflation and the pattern of demand, including the demand for imports? Would the amount which would be given to ailing industries be more than that taken away from healthy ones?

These unanswered questions serve to highlight the practicalities which prescriptions of this kind ignore. In short, tariffs by themselves would have been unlikely to have provided little more than a temporary palliative to ailing industries over the period under review.

More generally in relation to external dealings, the advantages which the City of London possesses as a major international financial centre were listed by the Wilson Committee: its historical role as centre of the *pax Britannica economica*; its geographical position close to Europe and between America and Asia; the overlap of its working day with those of both Europe and Asia; political stability; a high degree of integrity; a flexible regulatory system; a concentration of ancillary and cognate services; and the universality of the English language. Over many years these features have produced what might be termed tremendous institutional depth. For some, this depth is seen as having imposed an institutional bias and rigidity on the economy from as long ago as the late nineteenth century. Through its power and internal efficiency the City distorted the application of resources by channelling capital overseas at the expense of the domestic economy. Whatever the truth of such arguments, unquestionably City interests exercised a powerful influence on government policy up to 1939, most especially through that peculiarly English institution, the Bank of England. Nationalisation of the Bank in 1946 was a grand gesture of socialism in action but not an act which led to the capture of the commanding heights of finance. To the contrary, by bringing the Bank officially to the centre of policy-making while leaving the nature of the membership of its Court and the pattern of its recruitment largely unchanged, the Bank was allowed to do the capturing.

After the turmoils of the late 1940s the dominant objective of financial policy was the maintenance of sterling (Goodhart, 1973). In 1952 a scheme (known as ROBOT) was devised by the Treasury and the Bank of England for a floating rate of exchange for sterling and for the full convertibility of the currency subject to the funding of 80 per cent of the sterling balances held by non-dollar countries. Behind the scenes in Whitehall the scheme gave rise to protracted and contentious discussions. It is now clear that if the scheme had been adopted it would have had disastrous results. Fortunately, the plan was rejected (Cairncross, 1985). It would be interesting to know, however, whether the intensity of the debate at the time served to sear the official mind and closed it for many years afterwards to consideration of an alternative policy for sterling which substantially reduced its international role. Convertibility eventually came in 1958; but it came with a fixed exchange rate.

Henceforth, the Treasury and the Bank did not allow their minds to be troubled by questions about the proper role for sterling. They might thus be characterised as the two Ugly Sisters who through their actions succeeded in making the British economy the Cinderella of the industrialised world – and the USA could be cast as the Bad Fairy who ensured that the Ugly Sisters always got their way. Thus Susan Strange writes:

> My contention is that the main cause of the British predicament has not been the British economy but rather the decline of sterling and the failure of British policy to adapt to that decline . . . The United States had a strong direct interest in seeing that Britain did not try to solve its payments problems [in ways which] would have added to the burden on the United States (Strange, 1971, *318*).

The case against sterling is a powerful one (Hirsch, 1965). Balance of payments crises were met with 'stop/go' policies, involving credit squeezes and international borrowing which stunted economic growth. It was an approach introduced by the Conservatives in the 1950s and, in particular, exploited with consummate skill by Harold Macmillan, who used a 'go phase' to promote a consumer boom in time for the 1959 general election. Harold Wilson launched a fierce attack on 'stop/go' policy in 1964 with characteristic rhetoric. In effect he adopted the same methods to deal with worsening financial crises over the 1960s. Britain thus paid a heavy and increasing penalty for not having joined the European Economic Community in the early post-war period. But the charge that sterling policy was the main cause of the British predicament is more difficult to sustain, even if it is made part of a vicious circle of poor performance. Attention has been drawn to a range of influences which debilitated economic performance and it is hard, if not impossible, to see how the removal of the sterling burden would have significantly altered them. Why, for example, should it have improved product design or caused delivery dates to have been met? Moreover, there is a tendency to give too much weight to the destabilising effect of stop/go policies. Full employment (and the consequent high level of demand) over the medium and long term was a universal expectation during the years up to the late 1960s. So why was this condition not seen as giving prospects of profit and therefore providing adequate incentive to new investment which, in turn, would have strengthened the balance of payments and made sterling less of a handicap? Comparisons with other economies suggest that stop/go was not the problem, rather it was the weakness of the underlying trend of growth which exaggerated the effect of stop/go phases (Artis, 1972; Dow, 1964; Matthews, 1968). The short-lived benefits from the 1967 devaluation, and the persistence of poor economic performance after the floating of sterling in 1972, demonstrate not just the limited effect of devaluation but rather suggest that exchange rate difficulties are symptomatic of more fundamental problems (National Institute, 1972).

Strange's study (1971) of sterling policy is, nevertheless, particularly valuable because it places finance within a framework of international relations and domestic political economy. It is now fairly clear, moreover, that political considerations, of not wishing to be seen as having 'destroyed the value of the pound sterling', were of major importance in the Labour government's initial resistance to devaluation in 1967 quite apart from powerful pressures against devaluation being exerted on it by the Bank of England (Tomlinson, 1985). By contrast contemporary economic analysis of exchange rate policy saw the choice of alternative rates merely as a technical problem involving the conundrums of relative elasticities and inflationary effects. Even so, Strange still sees the issue in macro terms – as something which would be responsive to a *general* alteration in policy. In this important respect, and in common with more formal economic analysis, her study fails to appreciate the need to gain a much fuller understanding of microeconomic behaviour; something which can be done only through detailed investigation of individual businesses and economic institutions (Major, 1979). Some economists on the left did link the demand for maintaining the existing sterling rate with the need for a supply-side restructuring economic policy. But their prescriptions were somewhat polemical in form and linked to demands for protection (Stewart, 1977). Demands to abandon an existing shibboleth in order to replace it with an even older one.

7
Government policy and economic orthodoxy

The election of a Conservative government in 1951 is generally taken to signify the triumph of Butskellism – a new, consensus economic policy personified by Gaitskell and Butler, successively Labour and Conservative chancellors of the exchequer (Morgan, 1984; Pelling, 1984). It was based on a fusion of the commitment to full employment and a desire to promote consumer choice. More prosaically, it meant the end of rationing and the adoption of demand management. New investigation is beginning to cast considerable doubt on this interpretation of events, however. As has been noted, just before Labour's defeat Gaitskell, himself, was preparing a programme based on a high degree of government intervention – a form of economic planning which had antecedents in Bevin's earlier hopes of turning the Ministry of Labour into a major policy-making body. Electoral defeat rendered the proposal still-born. But the issue remained unresolved within the Labour Party and was to surface again when it returned to power in the 1960s.

In 1954 Butler set the aim of a doubling of the standard of living within twenty-five years. This did not immediately lead to what might be defined as specific growth policies. Until the early 1960s 'free markets', full employment and the maintenance of the value of sterling, remained the central aims (Shonfield, 1959). The return to 'free markets' by 1955 is generally viewed as permissive in the sense that it resulted from the removal of the remainder of war and post-war restrictions. But this fails to recognise how the manner of the return powerfully conditioned attitudes and institutional behaviour. What was involved was a process which underwrote the macro-approach to domestic economic policy. Indeed, if it is possible to talk of a Keynesian revolution in economic policy, then there is a strong case for placing it in the early 1950s rather than around 1947. Although there was a potential for conflict between the other two policy aims, full employment and the protection of sterling, they were sustained because any necessary adjustments could be absorbed by the overall growth of the economy. Thus the transmutation of the political economy of the post-war years was complete.

As to the economic system itself, the new credo was 'the mixed economy' (Crosland, 1956). To its ideologues it was a superior form which embodied the best of both socialism and capitalism. In mundane economic terms it meant the coexistence of public and private sectors. Once again, however, the ability of politicians and economists to conceptualise well outran their inclination to examine and analyse practical implications. Whilst millions of words were written on pricing policies and capital finance in nationalised industries, little serious thought was given to the economic relationships between the two sectors of the economy or to those between government and industry generally. Such matters were assumed away in the theory and waved away in the practice of macroeconomic management. Yet in relation to the needs of economic performance, the failures are now obvious. They came to roost in the late 1960s in the form of industrial decline and regional decay.

Keynesian economics was easily able to provide a suitable litany for the broad church of economic policy of the 1950s. It justified demand management but still contained sufficient neo-classical elements to satisfy adherents of the free market and the need for sound money. Until the early 1960s these beliefs were not seriously tested and differences of theory appear as shades of a fairly narrow spectrum. The public sector continued to grow through a process of bureaucratic accretion financed by economic growth. Over the 1950s and 1960s direct government expenditure on goods and services averaged 20 per cent of GDP to which has to be added a further 15 per cent in respect of transfer payments. Moreover, it is not without point that national economic consensus was at its strongest in the late 1950s under the premiership of Harold Macmillan. His belief in the politics of the middle way, which he had first expressed in the years of high unemployment in the 1930s, were easily reconstructed into modern Keynes-ianism.

Governments were supported by economic theorists in applying the prescriptions of short-term equilibrium analysis – and thereby supposedly maintaining at or near the full employment of re-sources – as the means for achieving long-term growth. But the connection between the short and the long run was a matter of belief and not of analysis. That it was misplaced belief was not adequately perceived because, as numerous statistics make clear, Britain's decline was relative and not absolute. Moreover, leading politicians, so committed to maintaining full employment, became deluded into thinking that the achievement of this target was direct proof of the maximisation of economic efficiency and social welfare.

Throughout the 1960s there was increasing analysis of and comment on what was seen to be Britain's flagging economic performance. Aspects of this have already been surveyed. In terms of government, the major issue is the effectiveness or otherwise of full employment policy (Worswick, 1970). These policies, many have argued, were hampered by a number of constraints, some of which – such as the sterling system –were self-imposed. There are, however, major conceptual problems involved in claims as to the desired level of GDP or the level which would have been achieved in the absence of discretionary intervention. But these aside, there is the straightforward practical question of why these constraints were allowed to persist. The commitment to sterling has already been examined in relation to the political economy of Britain's international role, the vested interests of the City of London and the nature of the system of government. The last, in particular, came in for detailed criticism in the 1960s and must, therefore, be considered a little further.

The attack was focused in the form of two official reports: *Control of Public Expenditure* (Plowden, 1961) and *The Civil Service* (Fulton, 1968). The former, while mainly concerned with the technicalities of Treasury operations, made a number of proposals relating to the functions of senior civil servants. In particular, it stressed the need for them to adopt a more professional approach to and an involvement in economic management as against the policy advisory role on which they exercised their intellects

(Brittan, 1971). The Fulton report was more specifically concerned with the recruitment and training of senior civil servants
and it was highly critical of the cult of the generalist and the
exclusive educational background which was the mark of the
mandarin (cf. Pliatzky, 1982). In particular, it added yet another
chapter of disapprobation on the theme of the narrow intelligence
and heavy hand of the Treasury within the government machine
(Barnett, 1982).

The failure of these investigations to yield practical results has
frequently been explained by abstruseness in the case of Plowden
and exaggerated analysis in the case of Fulton. Yet these explanations are only part of the story. Major reform depended on a
political will and competence strong enough either to coerce the
Treasury or to enlist its cooperation. These did not exist. And the
Treasury showed its true colours and relative power when its
economic authority was challenged by the government's attempt to
develop a more direct planning role through the formation of the
Department of Economic Affairs in 1964 under George Brown. By
time-honoured methods of mandarin machination the Treasury
succeeded in getting the Department abolished in 1969. The
Treasury's task was made easier by the unrealistic but much
heralded target of the National Plan, produced by the Department,
to achieve an annual growth rate of 4 per cent. But it was pretext
covering intent for all that (Opie, 1972).

In the sagas told of government economic policy up to the late
1960s, the natures of the heroes and villains vary according to the
teller, but there is an element common to many of them. It is the
emphasis on the role and potential effectiveness of macroeconomic
policy, in particular of demand management (Artis, 1972; Stewart,
1977). Domestic monetary policy, it is generally accepted, was
primarily determined by the defence of sterling by means of
interest-rate manipulation and credit control and, over the whole
period, was ineffective in controlling the money supply. The policy
was, therefore, broadly passive *per se* and the primary issue is its
stop/go effect, which was considered in the previous chapter (Artis,
1978, 1981; Clower, 1969; Croome and Johnson, 1970; Goodhart,
1973). So far as demand management is concerned, however, it is
now clear that from the 1950s to the mid 1960s budgets were
substantially in surplus and hence deflationary (Matthews, 1968).

The main *proximate* cause of high employment in comparison with interwar years was a comparatively high level of demand and investment though of course, governments contributed heavily to this through the public sector. A broader assessment of fiscal policy has concluded that it was positively destabilising but, as has been suggested above, this was probably of marginal significance (Dow, 1964; Blackaby, 1978). Moreover, while these analyses are useful in clarifying relationships the underlying explanation of them has to be sought in the factors surveyed by other chapters. What they do suggest indirectly, however, is that the economic rhetoric and even the orthodox economic beliefs of politicians bear nothing like a direct relationship to economic reality.

At all events the Treasury was opposed to new forms of central economic control (or planning) not least because they could well mean the loss of its own authority. Nevertheless, this attitude was probably not entirely a matter of hubris since the Treasury may well have had genuine doubts as to the potential effectiveness of planning (Brittan, 1971). There was, furthermore, the genuinely felt constitutional issue that planning by experts could mean a major reduction in the power of the Cabinet and Parliament. Even so, the conversion of Conservative chancellors to some form of planning – beginning with Selwyn Lloyd in 1960 – which led to the formation of the National Economic Development Council in 1962, represented a new element in economic policy (Polanyi, 1967). Under succeeding Labour governments in the 1960s demands for planning became more obtrusive in political rhetoric and in their practical aspects they involved the promotion of industrial reconstruction whether through mergers in the private sector or yet more reorganisation within the nationalised industries. It is noteworthy, however, that this was accompanied by a whole battery of macroeconomic instruments such as the Selective Employment Tax (1965). And in the late 1960s the over-riding concern switched to the circumstances surrounding the devaluation of 1967.

Most commentators agree that there was a change in ethos in economic policy over the 1960s which resulted in a more interventionist approach (Beckerman, 1972), and European practice was certainly an influence in bringing it about (Estrin and Holmes, 1983; Hayward and Narkiewicz, 1978; Shonfield, 1965). The

Industrial Reorganisation Corporation (1966) burgeoned in this atmosphere (Chapter 3). Yet the government as promoter at times conflicted with the government as regulator, particularly in the area of competition policy. Without doubt the former dominated the latter. But this made it extremely difficult to follow any strategy of industrial reorganisation; and in this respect there are interesting parallels between the late 1960s and the late 1940s. Even so, it would be too much to claim that the government possessed a carefully considered industrial strategy. The nearest it came to one was the abortive National Plan. The only sense in which the government had an overall strategy was in its continued determination to maintain full employment so far as was consistent with a fixed exchange rate. Accordingly, in many cases industrial intervention was a jobs-first and jobs-only policy. Thus large companies and boards of nationalised industries were provided with enormous financial assistance enabling (or rather persuading) them to base their reorganisation on designated development areas which in many cases they would not otherwise have chosen, for reasons of both private and public benefit when judged over the longer run (Knight, 1974; Moore and Rhodes, 1973).

Politicians are creatures of the short run. This fact was reflected both in broad economic strategy and in policies of intervention. It also matched the analytical strengths of formal economic analysis and correspondingly economic rationalisation to support immediate political needs was readily at hand. Indeed, under Labour governments professional economists experienced – and probably enjoyed – more political limelight than at any time since the Second World War. During the 1970s, however, the whole basis of analysis shifted when what had been accepted as fundamental axioms were falsified by economic experience in the real world. Economic growth declined and for a while even became negative. Of more dramatic impact was the discovery that high inflation and rising unemployment were compatible. All the while public expenditure was rising with direct and transfer payments together accounting for nearly 50 per cent of GDP by the mid 1970s. The manner and nature of these developments in the 1970s is not the concern of this study. But the way in which they affected interpretations of government policy of the quarter-century after the war certainly is of interest (Artis and Lewis, 1981).

The theoretical position underlying these interpretations is broadly described as 'monetarism', a doctrine which owes a great deal to two prominent economists, Friedrich Hayek and Milton Friedman. Much of it is not new; and it is perhaps better described as 'market economics' (Brittan, 1975). The message is clear: government cannot deliver the goods. To some extent this could be interpreted literally. But in a more sophisticated sense it means that the level of unemployment 'is not controllable by variations in demand-management' (ibid., *96*). That level – known as the natural or sustainable rate – is determined by labour market policies. Beyond provisions for retraining, such policies do not involve interventionism but the removal of obstacles – including minimum wage laws and 'excessive' social welfare benefits – which inhibit the efficiency of labour markets and, in particular, real-wage adjustments. This line of argument is tied in with analysis which stresses the need to regulate the money supply in order to maintain stable prices, as the only sustainable form of growth policy. Attempts to lower unemployment by means of a boost to monetary demand will work through into an increasing rate of inflation because of sticky prices and wages and increasing expectations of inflation (i.e. there is an absence of a money illusion). Trade unions, public sector employment and fixed exchange rates are cast as *bêtes noires*; the first because of their wage monopoly power, the second because of its size and comparative insulation from market forces, and the last because it shields the labour force from the consequences of its own actions which would otherwise appear as inflationary import prices. The close affinity between 'market economics' and the thesis of 'too few producers' is obvious.

Such a brief survey cannot do full justice to the theoretical ramifications of 'market economics', but it should be sufficient to indicate how the new doctrine has been directed against the very basis of demand management as practised between 1950 and the early 1970s (Walters, 1978). Along the way, there have been some interesting recantations by erstwhile Keynesian economists whilst their still committed colleagues have been stimulated to mount a counter-attack (Brittan, 1975; Hicks, 1975; Meade, 1982; Shonfield, 1984). But behind such flurries in the econo-mists' dovecote lies the question of whether the new economics stands the test of evidence. At one level, market economics involves gross simplification and, in particular, misunderstands the nature of and essential need for the political process in the provision of a whole range of goods (public goods) such as education and health (Shonfield, 1984). More directly in terms of economic performance, the new approach appears on the one hand to beg a number of questions whilst, on the other hand, having much in common with a Keynesian view of the world which it so frequently berates.

Market economics clearly makes a number of effective criticisms of demand management, and its emphasis on the limited competence of government to promote economic growth provides at least a valuable corrective to what became the orthodox political economy of the post-war period. However, one set of simplicities is dismissed only to be replaced by another. The central importance attached to the inefficiency of labour markets is either so generally abstract as to have little or no practical application or so partial as to ignore the necessary interdependence between labour supply and a whole range of institutions. Thus in the light of much which has been surveyed here, it is impossible to view overmanning – the bane of British industry – as mainly if not wholly the consequence of union power. The problem has had much to do with the quality of management and the nature of business organisation, themselves conditioned by various kinds of educational and legal provision. Again, the geographical mobility of labour – or lack of it – has often been determined by an inadequate supply of a range of new social overhead capital, particularly of housing. Only by engaging in extreme forms of economic casuistry can it be claimed that such things can be supplied satisfactorily without the agency of government at either national or local level.

Labour markets are indirectly affected by monopolistic competition in product markets. The power of producers to administer prices may reduce cost-consciousness and, in turn, the cost-efficiency with which labour is used. There is room for argument over the degree of monopolistic competition which is acceptable, but there is no serious challenge to the view that a substantial measure of concentration is a necessary feature of large areas of industry mainly because of the needs of technology and marketing. Precisely what effects this will have on the dynamics of the labour market is extremely complex but nonetheless real. It is certainly not something which can be simply removed.

The anti-institutional approach of market economics is, moreover, very narrowly conceived. The main concern is with organised labour and central government. Little or no account is taken of such corporate entities as manufacturers' associations, the City of London and the educational system; or of the whole range of institutions which sustain the British social system. Yet any comparison of British and foreign economic performance over the period since 1945 is soon brought up against the effects of different institutional forms. At this point the similarity between market economics and Keynesianism becomes apparent. They offer highly generalised solutions to complex problems of political economy. Although there is no necessary logical inconsistency between generality and complexity, in the British case at least the results of macroeconomic policies have not been impressive. Nevertheless, in their analysis of the effect of government policy on economic performance, market economists have learned far less than Keynesian economists from the accumulated evidence of the past hundred years. Politicians and civil servants have probably learned less than either of them.

The rise of monetarist economics was occasioned by the accelerating inflation of the late 1960s and the 1970s. Whilst it is generally agreed that increases in the money supply can cause higher prices, the question is through what mechanism does it operate? Monetarists have, moreover, failed to reconcile rising prices over the 1970s with decreasing demand pressure as registered by rising unemployment (Graham, 1979). If a much more severe monetary policy had been followed there is every reason to believe that while price rises would have been curtailed, unemployment would have risen even more sharply, thus confirming Keynesian analysis of a lack of aggregate demand rather than the monetarist concept of a natural rate of unemployment. Rising import prices – especially in the early 1970s – appear to have played an important part in the acceleration of price rises (Blackaby, 1979). The influence of wages is more difficult to assess because cause and effect are entangled with one another. Nevertheless, there are good grounds for thinking that the 'pay explosion' owed much to the institutional structure of British industrial relations (Phelps Brown, 1975).

Inflation had clearly supplanted economic growth as the major concern of government economic policy by the end of the period under review. The biggest problem was that British inflation was higher than the rates experienced by our major competitors. Britain's comparative failure to ride out international economic difficulties lends yet further weight to microeconomic causes in the explanation of its comparatively poor economic performance generally. The failure of successive governments to deal with these causes must be seen as a fundamental one.

8
Virtuous or vicious circles?

[handwritten annotations: hence "Golden Age" + "decline" / large gains alongside decline.]

Britain's poor economic performance has been the dominant theme of political debate and economic discourse since the 1950s. In one way this is surprising since the post-war record has been distinctly superior to the pre-war one: it took twenty-five years to double real wages in contrast to fifty years previously. Apart from income data, other quantifiable indicators – life expectancy, health, educational provision, hours of work, home ownership – show large gains (Halsey, 1972). Many of these changes have been directly related to progressive taxation, transfer payments and high levels of employment.

The interpretation of these changes in terms of economic welfare is not directly obvious, however, and raises a number of theoretical and conceptual issues. It is, for example, frequently assumed that more equal distribution of income and wealth raises the level of aggregate welfare (Atkinson, 1975). Philosophers from Aristotle through Bentham to Rawls (1971) have wrestled with the inner logic of equality. Even if one agrees with Aristotle that true equality consists in treating unequals unequally, this merely raises the apparently insoluble question of how it can be practically achieved. For Marxists, by contrast, the welfare of the masses is not only economically determined but a quantifiable function of the degree of their immiseration. In sharp contrast, others reject such determinism while emphasising the non-economic element in human welfare including such 'eternal verities of history that as societies become wealthy they are no longer able to afford pleasures that were well within their reach when they were poor' (F. J. Fisher, 'The Sixteenth and Seventeenth Centuries: The Dark Ages in English Economic History?', *Economica*, 24, 1957, 3). Of more practical importance, whether in government policy or historical interpretation, is the problem of how to strike the balance between the short and long run: the choice between more bread now or more bread *and* jam later. Yet even this is further complicated by changing (and almost inevitably rising) levels of expectations. Indeed, a striking feature of post-war economic growth has been the increasing importance of techniques of persuasion: only by stimulating wants and keeping consumers in a state of dissatisfaction is it possible to secure high levels of demand for much of the output of modern industrial economies. At the extreme this engenders a sense of relative deprivation which it is now fashionable to take as the measure of poverty.

One thing is clear: the test of performance in a modern industrial society is strongly concerned with the degree to which wants are satisfied in relative terms. In part this means in relation to other members of society as conditioned by the distribution of income and the operation of political power. In post-war democratic states this is particularly associated with a high degree of equality of distribution in comparison with earlier periods, and in this way lends plausibility to the assumption that greater equality means greater welfare. In part, however, performance is also measured by comparison with other economies. Hence Britain has suffered increasingly from an international demonstration effect since the Second World War.

Until the mid or even the late 1950s these comparisons were made mainly in a discrete way in the belief that advantages shifted from time to time between one country and another (Postan, 1967). By the 1960s, however, they were being interpreted in a continuous and cumulative manner which drew out their seriousness for the British economy. Britain was declared by a number of economists – in the language of divination rather than of positive science – to have entered a vicious circle of low growth and low productivity in contrast to the opposing virtuous relationship to be observed in France, Germany and Japan, in particular (Beckerman, 1979). The elaborate armoury of econometrics was used to refine, to form and reform, identities and correlates between logically separable elements of economic performance. But all this intellectual effort did not produce the key for turning vice into virtue (Cairncross, 1970a; Posner, 1978).

A more specific and strongly favoured analysis was based on 'Verdoorn's Law' (Verdoorn, 1949) which stated that there was a strong linear relationship between the rate of growth of labour productivity and the rate of growth of output. Kaldor (1966) in particular developed both theoretical analysis and official advice on the alleged connection (Kaldor, 1966, 1968, 1975). However, more comprehensive analysis of a range of economies was able to falsify the hypothesis (Rowthorn, 1975). Moreover, in the crucial sector of manufacturing output, whilst the rate of growth of output was the same between the pre- and post-war periods the rate of growth of total factor productivity grew 50 per cent faster in the latter period than in the earlier one (Matthews *et al.*, 1982). Such an order of difference is compelling. In some ways 'Kaldor's Law' could be seen as a re-statement of Say's Law: supply creates its own demand. But the only obvious truth of this kind in the UK has been that foreign supply creates domestic demand, the measure of which is import penetration.

In failing to match their forebodings about vicious circles with effective solutions for breaking them, economists risk being played at their own game. When the UK is compared with Western European economies and Japan there appears to be a strong inverse relationship between the number of economists acting as official government advisers and the rate of economic growth. It is, of course, a mere correlation. Good economic advice is important by definition; but what is its nature (Cairncross, 1970b; Cairncross, F., 1981)? Very little work has been done in this field but there has been sufficient to reveal that the refinement of economic theory (especially in terms of mathematical sophistication) is akin to fashioning scalpels to cut through jungle when it comes to the real world of policy-making (Graham, 1975). Governments, like theoretical economists, tend to be mainly concerned with the short run. The judgements of both are value-laden. There is, however, a crucial difference. Governments operate in the world of real time during which many elements can change, as against the economist's world of rational time and *ceteris paribus*. Add to this the complexity of the political system, with its perversities and special interests, and the potential power of economic logic is reduced to a low order.

The effectiveness of economic advice is but part of a larger problem: the appropriateness of the government machine to the tasks which have been placed upon it. Basic measures of the percentage of GNP passing through government hands in the form of direct expenditure (27 per cent in 1975) or transfer payments (22 per cent in 1975), the scale of the public sector and the battery of regulatory control, add up to an order of central economic direction which, by comparison, makes the Victorian age appear as one of pure *laissez-faire*. Some commentators assert a direct causal relationship between such dominance and the British disease of low productivity and slow economic growth (Bacon and Eltis, 1974). But in itself, the charge is not immediately convincing since similar degrees of central economic control can be observed for the fast-growing industrial economies. And there is strong historical evidence of a substantial increase in the scale of economic activities being an essential element in the development of modern economies and that an increasing government role is inherently a part of the process. The question thus becomes one of why other countries have been more successful than Great Britain in meeting these requirements.

The claim is sometimes made of a lack of continuity in policy which has been damaging to growth: in particular, that political changes have inhibited consistent action by civil servants. But the record does not bear this out: as our survey of the evidence has shown, persistence of basic economic aims and of common responses has been the order of the day through successive changes in government. It may well be the case, however, that to some degree fear of political change does inhibit civil servants, so that in order to ensure continuity they will only promote policies which they judge both major parties will accept. Thus there is continuity of policy but it is continuity on the lowest common factor.

New policies – in particular the move to interventionist industrial policy in the 1960s – were, for all their political rhetoric, often in the nature of additions to existing ones rather than changes in them. Changes have occurred but they have generally done so gradually over much longer intervals than changes of government – in part as a result of changes in official thinking, in larger part through alterations in the complex relationships between economic ideas, political ideology and the force of economic circumstance.

Hence, to ascribe the discernible shift in the 1970s to so-called monetarism to the force of domestic political change is to confuse cause with effect. The decline of US post-war economic hegemony, the oil price rise, the onset of stagflation: these were the forces which occasioned a new domestic political response. And the essential truth of Keynes's aphorism that an economic scribbler can be found to justify any course of action, was once again clearly demonstrated (Buchanan and Wagner, 1977). Economics, on this showing, has more practical use as ideology than as prescriptive science.

When economists describe Britain's relative economic decline since the Second World War as the outcome of a vicious circle of low growth and low productivity, they are employing a seductive metaphor and not providing a convincing explanation. More sober, technical economic analysis has provided much understanding of what we have termed proximate causes of economic performance but not of fundamental causes. Accordingly the major contribution of economics to policy over this period has been in providing some short-term corrections to economic activity whilst being able to do little to alter the long-term trend. So what does our analysis tell us about the underlying, or basic causes of the so-called 'British disease'?

Our survey has shown that there is no directly obvious and unequivocal explanation of Britain's economic performance. Indeed, the large literature on the subject is a reflection of the intractability of the problem. Nevertheless, some influences stand out and, in our view, of particular importance are the nature and operation of certain institutions. This is not to argue in terms of structuralism but in terms of a combination of institutional form and individual behaviour – elements which are bundled together as either part of *ceteris paribus* or part of the residual in factor productivity analyses.

Business organisation and management stand out as major causal weaknesses in UK economic performance. And, within business, our analysis has drawn attention to the role of financial institutions centred on the City of London. In particular, the apparent success in the field of invisible earnings may well be revealed after more careful investigation to be an outstanding case of private gain achieved at the expense of considerable social cost.

There is certainly accumulating circumstantial evidence to suggest that this is in fact the case. More broadly, the analysis has drawn attention to relationships between business organisation, the educational system and dominant social and cultural values. At the same time, these are obviously complex matters which require much more detailed examination.

It is tempting to place union organisation and practices in parallel to business organisation and management in an explanation of Britain's comparative economic weakness. There is, indeed, much evidence to support such a view, especially on the corrosive effects of overmanning on productivity; practices which spring from fusion of innate conservatism and the creed of job protection. On the evidence to date, however, there are grounds for judging unions in relation to management as slightly the lesser sinners. Union attitudes have been powerfully conditioned by long and bitter experience. Before 1914 workers suffered from employers' determination and ability (in a situation of a plentiful labour supply) to maintain low money wages regardless of the costs in terms of low productivity and slow adaptation to new technological possibilities. Between the world wars major unions suffered the searing experience of high unemployment which owed much to incompetent employers and benighted policy-makers. These experiences do not, of course, wholly explain modern union behaviour or remove from unions much of the responsibility for changing matters.

The higher civil service has been accused by many writers of being a major cause of Britain's weak economic performance (Allen, 1976). It is an accusation which this analysis fully supports. The indictment includes slowness in decision-making, a vested interest in avoiding change, the deleterious influence of the Treasury and inappropriate training. The top echelons of the civil service have generally abjured responsibility for policy decisions. Yet as the evidence is unfolded it becomes increasingly incongruous that the mandarins of Whitehall should claim so little when they patently control so much. Moreover, top civil servants are not only involved in policy formation. They are frequently directly responsible for its execution. Of the charges which have been made against the civil service, those against the Treasury have probably been the most substantial (Brittan, 1971). Its central role in policy-making has already been considered. Less immediately obvious has been its powerful influence on the training and recruitment of the civil service for most of the period under review. Thus, for all the vast growth in the range of government activities – which has meant that civil servants have effectively been making major business decisions on the allocation of resources – the Treasury made little attempt to devise fundamentally new and appropriate methods of training and re-training (Fulton Report, 1968; Chapman and Greenaway, 1980). Perhaps a telling comment on this is that a major reason for the recruitment of top, super-annuated civil servants into business is that they know their way round the political labyrinth of Whitehall. In general, it is impossible to measure the economic cost of our system of administration. But the distinctiveness of the British higher civil service in comparison with the systems which operate among our major competitors, at the very least amounts to powerful circumstantial evidence against it (Postan, 1967).

In sum, there are strong grounds for arguing that, together with business organisation and management, the higher civil service has been a major cause of Britain's comparatively poor economic performance. The closest points of contact between the two elements have been the Treasury and the Bank of England. During the period under review the top cadres of business and government administration have been drawn predominantly from similar social and educational backgrounds. Whatever qualities of leadership are bred by English public schools, that of successful economic leadership is clearly not among them (Barnett, 1986).

For all their probable weaknesses, however, the civil service, business and the unions do not have a monopoly of conservatism and resistance to change. Attention has been drawn above to the economic implications of similar problems in relation to education and foreign policy, though in both cases the civil service is a closely involved party. Moreover, if the perspective is lengthened to include the Victorian period the observer cannot fail to be struck by a feeling of historical *déjà vu* (Kirby, 1981). In this light, the educational reforms of the post-1945 years appear less radical than has frequently been claimed (Addison, 1977). For example, the relationship between education and economic need – which had for long been a matter of concern in Britain and the object of telling comparisons with Germany and the USA – was never fundamentally tackled (Robbins, 1963). Excellence continued to be defined in terms of intellectual capacity in theoretical or abstract analysis and not in terms of the practical application of knowledge. The study of economics provides a classic example. The dynamics of the relationship between education and economic performance are far from clear, however. In Germany the nature of the educational system has been in tune with both the needs of industry and prevailing social values (Locke, 1984). A practical consequence of this relationship has been that from the late nineteenth century onwards managerially and technically trained personnel have been well represented on the boards of major German companies. In Britain, by contrast, prevailing social values have conditioned the educational system to inculcate the belief that manufacturing is an inferior form of economic activity. It may well be a belief which has been, and still is, widely shared by top industrialists themselves. Accordingly it is interesting to speculate to what extent these attitudes have caused British businessmen to adopt short time-horizons in making decisions – with negative consequences for longer-term growth performance – because their main objective is to acquire sufficient wealth to enable them to move on to the better things in life.

Understandably, in the light of its heroic effort in 1940 and its enormous contribution to the subsequent defeat of the fascist enemy, Britain mistook being on the winning side for having won the war. This attitude contributed to serious misjudgements in the immediate post-war period because it was not counteracted by radical institutional change as a result of the war. Such lack of fundamental change is perhaps understandable because, since the eighteenth century, the rate of economic growth in Britain has been slow, a rate which influenced and was influenced by the nature of the institutional and social system. The result has been to produce a society of great institutional depth. Thus, it was the accustomed pace of change rather than the fact of an early start, which had already begun to place Britain at a disadvantage in competition against her major rivals at the beginning of the present century. That the rate of growth accelerated after 1945 is some measure of the impact of the Second World War; but to the question of whether the institutional changes this embodied were enough to match the requirements of rapid economic growth, the answer is clearly no.

Explanation of Britain's relative economic decline in the third quarter of the twentieth century remains elusive. In itself this elusiveness is testimony to just how enormously difficult it is to find practical solutions to Britain's economic problems.

Select bibliography

This is a selective bibliography even though its length may appear to belie the fact. There is an enormous amount of literature bearing on the subject, especially from the areas of theoretical and applied economics. By contrast there is, as yet, much less which attempts to interpret Britain's post-war economic development within a framework of historical analysis. Furthermore, the literature encompasses a wide range of levels of difficulty. Accordingly, I have indicated basic, essential reading with an asterisk.

Place of publication is London unless otherwise indicated.

[1] Aaronvitch, S. and Sawyer, M. C. (1975) *Big Business: Theoretical and Empirical Aspects of Concentration and Mergers in the U.K.* Contains much useful data and analysis.

[2] Addison, P. (1977) *The Road to 1945.* Endeavours to make the case for the emergence of a reforming concensus between the major political parties over the war period.

[3] Alford, B. W. E. (1976) 'The Chandler Thesis – Some General Observations' in Leslie Hannah (ed.), *Management Strategy and Business Development.* Discusses the problems of analysing structure and performance in large companies.

[4] Allen, G. C. (1976) *The British Disease. A Short Essay on the Nature and Causes of the Nation's Lagging Wealth.* A vigorous critique by an economist with wide-ranging interests and experience, which emphasises the need for radical changes in attitudes and institutions.*

[5] Allsopp, C. J. (1979) 'The Management of the World Economy', in Beckerman (ed.) [22]. Valuable account of the international factors conditioning post-war growth.*

[6] Arndt, H. W. (1978) *The Rise and Fall of Economic Growth.* Described as a study in economic thought it is, more accurately, an interesting

analysis of the relationship between economic theory and economic ideology.

[7] Artis, M. J. (1972) 'Fiscal Policy for Stabilization', in Beckerman (ed.) [21]. Together with the following two items, this provides a survey of monetary and fiscal policy.

[8] Artis, M. J. (1978) 'Monetary Policy', in Blackaby (ed.) [26]. Brings out the largely passive nature of monetary policy over the period 1960–74.*

[9] Artis, M. J. and Lewis, M. K. (1981) *Monetary Control in the U.K.* A basic analysis of policy and the mechanism through which it is operated.

[10] Artus, J. R. (1975) 'The 1967 Devaluation of the Pound Sterling', *International Monetary Fund Staff Papers*, 223. A best-estimate of the effects of devaluation.

[11] Ashworth, W. (Oxford, 1986) *History of the British Coal Industry. Vol. 5. The Nationalized Industry 1945–1982.* The major work on a major industry.

[12] Atkinson, A. B. (Oxford, 1975) *The Economics of Inequality.* The best and most comprehensive analysis in this field.

[13] Bacon, R. W. and Eltis, W. A. (1974) *The Age of U.S. and U.K. Machinery.* A technical analysis which concludes that higher US productivity was not largely explained by superior plant. Points to less easily quantifiable or unquantifiable elements of managerial and labour practices as holding the key to the difference. But proportionately low investment in the US does not make it a good comparator.

[14] Bacon, R. and Eltis, W. A. (1976) *Britain's Economic Problem: Two Few Producers?* The thesis that claims on marketed output from outside the market sector were excessive. Important in the de-industrialisation debate, more for its political appeal than its analytical cogency.*

[15] Ball, R. J. (1967) 'The Case Against Devaluation of the Pound', *Bankers' Magazine*, 203. Stresses the likely inflationary effects of devaluation.

[16] Barnett, C. (1972) *The Collapse of British Power.* A provocative analysis by a political historian.

[17] Barnett, C. (1986) *The Audit of War: the Illusion and Reality of Britain as a Great Nation.* A spirited analysis by a political historian which develops a number of themes parallel to those examined in this survey.

[18] Barnett, J. (1982) *Inside the Treasury.* A revealing study by a former Chief Secretary.

[19] Batchelor, R. A., Major, R. L. and Morgan, A. D. (Cambridge, 1980) *Industrialization and the Basis for Trade.* Contains useful

comparative data on the growth, pattern and composition of trade for the period.

[20] Bauer, P. T. and Walters, A. A. (1975) 'Economists and the Dollar Problem', *Lloyds Bank Review*, 116. Condemns fixed exchange rates. Fairly unrestrained monetarism and highly condemnatory of what they see as the political pliability of economic advisers.

[21] Beckerman, W. (ed.) (1972) *The Labour Government's Economic Record 1964–70*. A valuable though somewhat committed collection of essays around the theme of Labour's achievements. Nevertheless, there is clear recognition of failures in the fields of planning and, to a lesser degree, equality. Sterling is cast as the *bête noire*.

[22] Beckerman, W. (ed.) (1979) *Slow Growth in Britain. Causes and Consequences*. Essential reading.*

[23] Bell, P. W. (Oxford, 1956) *The Sterling Area in the Postwar World: Internal Mechanism and Cohesion*. Good critical analysis in both economic and political terms.

[24] Beynon, H. (1984 edn) *Working for Ford*. A controversial study of workers' attitudes by an industrial sociologist. It is set within a basically Marxist framework.

[25] Bhaskar, K. (1979) *The Future of the Motor Industry*. An in-depth study containing many useful data.

[26] Blackaby, F. T. (ed.) (Cambridge, 1978) *British Economic Policy 1960–74*. Carries on from where Dow leaves off. A basic reference work.*

[27] Blackaby, F. T. (ed.) (1979) *De-industrialization*. Essential reading.*

[28] Blaug, M. (1965) 'The Rate of Return on Investment in Education in Great Britain', *Manchester School*, 33. (Including an appendix by D. Henderson-Stewart.) Exemplifies the difficulties involved in such analyses.

[29] Bolton Report (1971) *Report of the Committee of Inquiry on Small Firms*, Cmnd. 4811. A *crie de coeur* in the cause of small firms. The report contains much useful information and makes a number of recommendations, which remain largely unfulfilled.

[30] Booth, A. (1983) 'The "Keynesian Revolution" in Economic Policy-Making', *Economic History Review*, 36. With the next item, a contribution to the debate on this issue.

[31] Booth, A. (1984) 'Defining a Keynesian Revolution', *Economic History Review*, 37.

[32] Brittan, S. (3rd edn, 1971) *Steering the Economy*. Informed and critical account of the Treasury role in the formulation of economic policy.*

[33] Brittan, S. (1975) *Second Thoughts on Full Employment Policy*. The recantation of a Keynesian who has now become a disciple of Milton Friedman. At least he proclaims the new message with characteristic clarity if not persuasiveness.

[34] Brown, A. J. (Cambridge, 1972) *The Framework of Regional Economies in the United Kingdom.* The standard work.

[35] Brown, C. J. F. and Sheriff, T. D. (1979) 'De-industrialization: a Background Paper' in Blackaby (ed.) [27]. Contains useful data on the main theme.*

[36] Brown, W. (ed.) (Oxford, 1981) *The Changing Contours of British Industrial Relations. A Survey of Manufacturing Industry.* A survey based on the late 1970s but makes valuable comparisons with studies on earlier periods.

[37] Buchanan, M. J. and Wagner, R. E. (1977) *Democracy in Deficit. The Political Legacy of Lord Keynes.* A provocative and stimulating attack on 'Keynesianism' from the 'New Right', though it relates mainly to the political economy of the USA.

[38] Bullock, A. (1983) *Ernest Bevin: Foreign Secretary 1945–51.* The third volume of this classic biography by a master of the art. Important insights into Bevin's attitude towards Europe in both political and economic terms.

[39] Cairncross, A. (ed.) (1970a) *Britain's Economic Prospects Reconsidered.* Very useful collection of essays covering different aspects of economic performance at the macro level.*

[40] Cairncross. A. (Oxford, 1970b) *The Managed Economy.* A critical view of the process of economic policy-making; though the redoubtable Keynesian shows through.

[41] Cairncross, A. (1985) *Years of Recovery. British Economic Policy 1945–51.* Particularly useful on the international aspects. Overall gives the Labour government high marks for achievement thought it is very questionable whether he establishes his case in either *ex ante* or *ex post* terms.*

[42] Cairncross, A. and Eichengreen, B. (Oxford, 1983) *Sterling in Decline.* An examination of the political economy of the devaluations of 1931, 1949 and 1967.

[43] Cairncross, A., Kay, J. A. and Silberston, A. (Autumn, 1977) 'The Regeneration of Manufacturing Industry', *Midland Bank Review.* Useful survey of the main issues.*

[44] Cairncross, F. (ed.) (1981) *Changing Perceptions of British Economic Policy.* Essays and comments by former official economic advisers. As much to be gained from reading between the lines as from the lines themselves.*

[45] Carter, C. F. (ed.) (1981) *Industrial Policy and Innovation.* Useful articles on these themes.

[46] Caves, R. (ed.) (Washington, DC, 1968) *Britain's Economic Prospects.* An economic 'health scan' conducted by members of the Brookings Institute. Essential reading.*

[47] Caves, R. and Krause, L. (eds) (Washington, DC, 1980) *Britain's*

Economic Performance. A follow-up to the previous report, though the focus is narrower. The diagnosis is still as gloomy.*

[48] Central Policy Review Staff (CPRS) (1975) *The Future of the British Car Industry.* A 'think-tank' report. Provides much valuable statistical information on an international, comparative basis.

[49] Channon, D. F. (1973) *The Strategy and Structure of British Enterprise.* Indispensable study of the development of modern company organisation.*

[50] Chapman, R. A. and Greenaway, J. R. (1980) *The Dynamics of Administrative Reform.* A useful, mainly narrative, account which indirectly brings out the lack of dynamism in the process.

[51] Chester, D. N. (1975) *The Nationalization of British Industry 1945–51.* An exhaustive record of the manner and form of nationalisation, industry by industry.

[52] Clark, T. A. and Williams, N. P. (1978) 'Measures of Real Profitability', *Bank of England Quarterly,* 18. Emphasises that the accelerating decline in the 1970s has to be seen against a longer downward trend beginning around 1960.

[53] Clarke, R. W. B. (Oxford, 1982) *Anglo-American Collaboration in War and Peace 1942–49.* Particularly valuable as an insight into a civil servant's view of policy and policy-makers.*

[54] Clegg, H. A. (Oxford, 1972) *The System of Industrial Relations in Great Britain.* The standard work.*

[55] Clower, R. W. (ed.) (1969) *Monetary Theory.* A useful and not too theoretically forbidding text.

[56] Cockerill, A. and Silberston, A. (Cambridge, 1974) *The Steel Industry. International Comparisons of Industrial Structure and Performance.* An in-depth analysis of economies of scale in which the UK shows up badly against a not altogether high standard.

[57] Coleman, D. C. (1973). 'Gentleman and Players', *Economic History Review,* 26. An elegant analysis of boardroom ethos and recruitment in British business.*

[58] Coleman, D. C. (Oxford, 1980) *Courtaulds. An Economic and Social History. Vol. 3. Crisis and Change 1940–1965.* Contains much of interest on company strategy and an in-depth analysis of a major takeover bid – that of ICI for Courtaulds in 1962.

[59] Conan, A. R. (1961) *The Rationale of the Sterling Area.* Documents and commentary. Generally favourable to the system.

[60] Cripps, F. and Godley, W. (1978) 'Control of Imports as a Means to Full Employment and the Expansion of World Trade: the U.K.'s Case', *Cambridge Journal of Economics,* 2. The case for tariffs as a cure for de-industrialisation.

[61] Croome, D. R. and Johnson, H. G. (eds) (1970) *Money in Britain 1959–69.* A useful survey of theory and empirical data.

[62] Crosland, A. (1967) *The Future of Socialism*. The classical political statement for the mixed economy and of the manner in which socialists need to come of age as social democrats.

[63] Cyert, R. M. and March, J. G. (New Jersey, 1963) *A Behavioural Theory of the Firm*. Still the best antidote to the marginal theory and, indirectly, makes the case for much more business history.

[64] Day, A. C. L. (Oxford, 1954) *The Future of Sterling*. A major critique of the system.

[65] Denison, E. F. (Washington, DC, 1986) *Why Growth Rates Differ: Postwar Experience in Nine Western Countries*. The classic work in factor productivity analysis.

[66] Donovan Report (1968) *Royal Commission on Trade Unions and Employers' Associations 1965–1968. Report*. Cmnd. 3623. Contains much useful information. Concentrates on immediate ways of improving industrial relations but does not deal with the longer term position of trade unions within a democratic society.

[67] Dore, R. P. (1973) *British Factory – Japanese Factory: The Origins of National Diversity in Industrial Relations*. Particularly revealing on differing labour attitudes.

[68] Dornbusch, R. and Fisher, S. (1980) 'Sterling and the External Balance', in Caves and Krause (eds) [46]. A broad survey which brings out the major issues.*

[69] Dow, J. C. R. (Cambridge, 1964) *The Management of the British Economy 1945–60*. A mine of information and a generally sceptical assessment of the effectiveness of government policy.*

[70] Dunning, J. H. (1979) 'The U.K.'s International Direct Investment Position in the mid-1970s', *Lloyds Bank Review*, 132. Brings out the rise in the manufacturing sector, against the general trend. Argues for measures to improve the locational attractions of the UK for investment and against controls on overseas investment.

[71] Eckes, A. E. Jr. (1975) *A Search for Solvency: Bretton Woods and the International Monetary System*. Useful general account.

[72] *Economic Trends* (Monthly/Cumulative) Essential source for main statistical data on the economy.

[73] Eltis, W. (1979) 'How Rapid Public Sector Growth Can Undermine the Growth of the National Product', in Beckerman (ed.) [22]. The case stated.

[74] Employment Policy (1944) *White Paper on Employment Policy*. Cmd. 6527. The official manifesto of full employment.

[75] Estrin, S. and Holmes, P. (1983) *French Planning in Theory and Practice*. Useful for narrative information rather than for the prescriptions it offers.

[76] Feinstein, C. H. (Cambridge, 1972) *National Income, Expenditure and Output of the United Kingdom, 1856–1965*. The standard work.

[77] Fetherston, M., Moore, B. and Rhodes, J. (1977) 'Manufacturing Export Shares and Cost Competitiveness of Advanced Industrial Countries', *Economic Policy Review*, 3. Estimates which stress residual as against price factors. Provides a rough measure of Britain's 'lost world'.

[78] Flemming, J. S. *et al.* (1976). 'The Cost of Capital, Finance and Investment', *Bank of England Quarterly Bulletin*, 16. Demonstrates how the fall in the cost of finance over the 1960s and the partial return in the early 1970s was outstripped by the fall in profits. As part of their assessment of the effect on investment they provide a clear survey of relevant theory.

[79] Freeman, C. F. (1979) 'Technical Innovation and British Trade Performance', in Blackaby (ed.) [27]. Useful, internationally comparative data of R & D expenditure.*

[80] Friedman, A. L. (1977) *Industry and Labour. Class Struggle at Work and Monopoly Capitalism*. A microeconomic analysis of alleged capitalist exploitation in which technological change is seen as a tool of managerial control over labour.

[81] Fulton Report (1968) *The Civil Service*. Cmd. 3638. An important but little heeded critique of the civil service. Many of its proposals are still apposite and still steadfastly resisted by the civil service establishment.

[82] Gardner, R. N. (1969 edn) *Sterling–Dollar Diplomacy*. A fascinating and perceptive study first published in 1956, but this edition contains a broad and sobering survey of the period up to the late 1960s.*

[83] Godley, W. (1979) 'Britain's Chronic Recession: Can Anything Be Done?', in Beckerman (ed.) [22]. The case for tariffs.

[84] Gomulka, S. (1979) 'Increasing Efficiency Versus Low Rate of Technical Change', in Beckerman (ed.) [22]. An excellent article. More work in this field is urgently needed.*

[85] Goodhart, C. A. E. (Boston, USA, 1973) 'Monetary Policy in the United Kingdom', in K. Holbik (ed.), *Monetary Policy in Twelve Industrial Countries*. Excellent survey for 1957–67 within a crystal clear conceptual framework. Emphasises high interest rate policy for sterling and inability to control the money supply.*

[86] Graham, A. W. (Cambridge, 1975) 'Impartiality and Bias in Economics', in A. Montefiore (ed.), *Neutrality and Impartiality*. Why economics and politics cannot be separated.

[87] Graham, A. W. (1979) 'Inflation', in D. Morris [130]. A clear survey of the theoretical issues and empirical evidence for most of the period.*

[88] Halsey, A. H. (ed.) (1972) *Trends in British Society Since 1900*. Extremely valuable collection of statistics arranged by topics with specialist commentaries.

[89] Hannah, L. (1982) *Engineers, Managers, and Politicians: The First Fifteen Years of Nationalized Electricity Supply in Britain.* A detailed record of how the industry was run and how major decisions were made.

[90] Hannah, L. and Kay, J. A. (1977) *Concentration in Modern Industry: Theory, Measurement and the U.K. Experience.* The best study on manufacturing industry. Differs in major respects from Hart and Clarke [94] and Prais (1976) [155].

[91] Harris, J. (1977) *William Beveridge: A Biography.* A first-class study which reveals much about the formulation of social welfare policy.

[92] Harris, J. (1981) 'Some Aspects of Social Policy Making in Britain During the Second World War', in W. J. Mommsen (ed.), *The Emergence of the Welfare State in Britain.* Useful background discussion of the issues.

[93] Harris, R. and Sewill, B. (1975) *British Economic Policy 1970–74: Two Views.* Monetary policy versus stronger control of trade unions as cures for Britain's economic ills. They are, however, neither exclusive nor necessarily valid despite the assertiveness of the authors.

[94] Hart, P. E. and Clarke, R. (Cambridge, 1980) *Concentration in British Industry, 1935–75.* Differs in method and conclusion from Hannah and Kay. In particular, gives far less weight to the influence of merger activity.

[95] Hayward, J. and Narkiewicz, O. (eds) (1978) *Planning in Europe.* Covers both eastern and western Europe. Useful as a source of factual information for comparisons with the UK.

[96] Hicks, J. (1975) 'What is Wrong with Monetarism', *Lloyds Bank Review*, 118. A good dose of common sense.

[97] Hirsch, F. (1965) *The Pound Sterling: a Polemic.* A stimulating attack on the sterling system.*

[98] HMSO (1980) *An A to Z of Income and Wealth.* Provides a very clear summary of the findings of the *Royal Commission on the Distribution of Income and Wealth* (Diamond Commission).

[99] Hughes, J. J. and Thirlwall, A. P. (1977) 'Trends and Cycles in Import Penetration in the U.K.', *Oxford Bulletin of Economics and Statistics*, 39. In-depth analysis which, in particular, demonstrates the ratchet effect of import penetration.

[100] Jones, D. T. (1976) 'Output, Employment and Labour Productivity in Europe since 1955', *National Institute Economic Review*, 77. An extremely valuable analysis.*

[101] Jones, R. and Marriott, O. (1970) *Anatomy of a Merger: the History of G.E.C., A.E.I. and English Electric.* Financial journalism at its best.

[102] Kaldor, N. (Cambridge, 1966) *Causes of the Slow Rate of Growth of*

the United Kingdom. A sophisticated polemic which argued that the UK's growth was low because of a low rate of growth of labour available for manufacturing industry. Provoked critical analysis which exposed its fallacies. See in particular the articles by Gomulka [84] and Rowthorne [170].

[103] Kaldor, N. (1968) 'Productivity and Growth in Manufacturing Industry: A Reply', *Economica*, 35. Part of the same controversy.

[104] Kaldor, N. (1971) 'Conflicts in National Economic Objectives', *Economic Journal*, 81. The case for demand management which concentrates on export-led growth as against internal demand.

[105] Kaldor, N. (1975) 'Economic Growth and the Verdoorn Law', *Economic Journal*, 85. An attempt to rely to Rowthorne [170].

[106] Kay, J. and King, M. (Oxford, 1978) *The British Tax System*. The standard work.

[107] Keynes, J. M. (1946) 'The Balance of Payments of the United States', *Economic Journal*, 56. Develops the argument that there would be no fundamental, post-war dollar problem. Even Homer nods.

[108] King, M. (1975) 'The United Kingdom Profits Crisis: Myth or Reality?', *Economic Journal*, 85. By means of a careful examination of tax provisions and accounting procedures, effectively challenges the claim that profits fell sharply.

[109] Kirby, M. W. (1981) *The Decline of British Economic Power*. A useful general survey.

[110] Knight, A. (1974) *Private Enterprise and Government Intervention*. An interesting account by an industrialist whose company (Courtaulds) was much affected by government industrial policy.

[111] Kravis, I. B. (1976) 'A Survey of International Comparisons of Productivity', *Economic Journal*, 86. Despite the enormous problems involved in exercises of this kind, the UK's declining relative position is clear.

[112] Kregel, J. A. (1972) *The Theory of Economic Growth*. A clear introduction to modern theories for the non-specialist.

[113] Law, C. M. (1980) *British Regional Development since World War I*. A basic text which comprehensively surveys the literature.

[114] Locke, R. R. (Greenwich, Connecticut, 1984) *The End of Practical Man: Entrepreneurship and Higher Education in Germany, France and Great Britain*. Exceptionally good on the German case but generalises too much from it. Does not adequately consider the dynamics of the relationship between education and industrial performance.

[115] London and Cambridge Economic Service (1970) *The British Economy, Key Statistics 1900–1970*. Compact source of basic data.*

[116] Louis, W. R. (1977) *Imperialism at Bay 1941–1945: The United States and the Decolonisation of the British Empire*. Brings out the

inherent sense of imperial destiny in British politics and the USA's deep suspicion of it.

[117] MacLennan, D. and Parr, J. (eds) (1979) *Regional Policy: Past Experience and New Directions.* An informative survey which covers the historical, policy and theoretical aspects of regional economic development.

[118] Maddison, A. (1964) *Economic Growth in the West.* Still useful but perhaps of most interest as a period piece: demand and investment explain all – or nearly all.

[119] Maddison, A. (1982) *Phases of Capitalist Development.* A valuable survey – largely quantative – of the performances of the major economies since 1820.

[120] Major, R. J. (ed.) (1979) *Britain's Trade and Exchange Rate Policy.* Presents a full range of economists' views and, not unexpectedly, comes to no clear conclusion.

[121] Marris, R. (1964) *The Economic Theory of 'Managerial' Capitalism.* A pioneering and classic attempt to develop an alternative to the sterile marginalist approach.

[122] Matthews, R. C. O. (1968) 'Why Has Britain Had Full Employment Since the War?', *Economic Journal*, 78. Demonstrates that fiscal policy was, on balance, deflationary. Gives little weight to external items (particularly exports). Emphasises the major contribution of investment.

[123] Matthews, R. C. O., Feinstein, C. H. and Odling-Smee, J. C. (Oxford, 1982) *British Economic Growth, 1856–1973.* The British equivalent of Denison [65]. Extremely valuable for the wide range of data it collects together.

[124] Meade, J. (1982) *Stagflation. Vol. I, Wage Fixing.* Beautifully clear statement of 'New Keynesianism'. Some readers of it may develop a strong sense of *déjà vu*.

[125] Meeks, G. (Cambridge, 1977) *Disappointing Marriage: A Study of the Gains from Merger.* Tests the prospectuses of takeovers and mergers against subsequent performance and finds them substantially unjustified. Argues the case for regulation of takeovers and mergers.

[126] Milard, A. S. (1984) *The Reconstruction of Western Europe 1945–51.* A controversial and stimulating analysis which lays stress on the political, as against the economic, reconstruction of Europe.

[127] Moore, B. and Rhodes, J. (1973) 'Evaluating the Effects of British Regional Policy', *Economic Journal*, 83, 87–110. Demonstrates how difficult such calculations are. Nevertheless, the study concludes that such policies have considerable potential.

[128] Moore, B. and Rhodes, J. (1976) 'The Relative Decline of the U.K. Manufacturing Sector', *Economic Policy Review*, 2. Useful data on

trade and import penetration. Various interventionist policy proposals.

[129] Morgan, K. O. (Oxford, 1984) *Labour in Power 1945–1951*. A detailed record and a favourable assessment which probably gives insufficient weight to economic criteria.*

[130] Morris, D. (ed.) (Oxford, 1979 edn). *The Economic System of the U.K.* Specialists examine various aspects of the economy within a framework of economic analysis which is 'user friendly'.*

[131] Morris, V. and Ziderman, A. (1971) 'The Economic Return on Investment in Higher Education in England and Wales', *Economic Trends*, 211. Cost-benefit calculations based on education costs and longitudinal salary data.

[132] National Institute (1972) 'Effects of the 1967 Devaluation', *Economic Journal*, 82. In particular, brings out the low export price elasticity of demand for manufactured goods. Invisibles fare better, but the total effect was not massive as many had predicted.

[133] Newton, C. C. S. (1984) 'The Sterling Crisis of 1947 and the British Response to the Marshall Plan', *Economic History Review*, 37. An attempt to argue that Britain's post-war international economic policies were based on sound judgements which were thwarted by the USA, not least through the Marshall Aid programme.

[134] Opie, R. (1972) 'Economic Planning and Growth', in Beckerman (ed.) [21]. A post-mortem on the National Plan (1965).

[135] Pagnamenta, P. and Overy, R. (1984) *All Our Working Lives*. Popular, illustrated account of the development of a number of industries since 1914. One of the few examples of effective use of oral information.*

[136] Paish, F. W. (1962) *Studies in an Inflationary Economy. The United Kingdom, 1948 to 1961*. Something of a period piece which expounds the author's credo.

[137] Paish, F. W. (1968) 'Inflation and the Balance of Payments in the United Kingdom 1952–1967', *Scottish Journal of Political Economy*, 15. Reprinted in F. W. Paish, *How the Economy Works*. The case for demand management in terms of maintaining a margin of unused capacity in order to avoid balance of payments crises.

[138] Panic, M. (1975) 'Why the U.K.'s Propensity to Import is High', *Lloyds Bank Review*, 115. Important basic analysis of the data.*

[139] Panic, M. (ed.) (1976) *The U.K. and West German Manufacturing Industry 1954–72*. Excellent empirical work which shows that the countries have very similar industrial structures but that Britain's operative ability is frighteningly inferior in all departments.

[140] Pavitt, K. (ed.) (1980) *Technical Innovation and British Economic Performance*. A wide-ranging collection of essays covering general issues and specific examples.

[141] Peck, M. J. (1968) 'Science and Technology' in Caves (ed.) [46]. Excellent analysis of research and development expenditure and the use of scientific manpower.*

[142] Peden, G. C. (1987) *Keynes, The Treasury and British Economic Policy*. Valuable for its survey of the debate over 'Keynesianism'.*

[143] Pelling, H. (1984) *The Labour Governments 1945–51*. Useful, mainly narrative account of the political history of the period.

[144] Phelps Brown, E. H. (1975) 'A Non-Monetarist View of the Pay Explosion', *Three Banks Review*, 105. A perceptive analysis of changing trade union attitudes.*

[145] Phelps Brown, E. H. (1977) 'What is the British Predicament?', *Three banks Review*, 116. An outstandingly good analysis of 'non-economic' factors in Britain's relative economic decline.*

[146] Phillips, A. W. (1958) 'The Relation Between Unemployment and the Rate of Change in Money Wage Rates in the U.K. 1861–1957', *Economica*, 25. A classic article in terms of what it set in train both in the literature and policy.

[147] Pliatzky, L. (Oxford, 1982) *Getting and Spending: Public Expenditure, Employment and Inflation*. Somewhat chatty and superficial but indirectly revealing for all that.

[148] Plowden Report (1961) *The Control of Public Expenditure* Cmnd. 1432. A major enquiry though it is far from easy reading.

[149] Polanyi, G. (1967) *Planning in Britain: The Experience of the 1960s*. An attack on contemporary efforts at planning. Somewhat jaundiced but contains useful information.

[150] Pollard, S. (1982) *The Wasting of British Economy*. Polemical in tone and stresses the poor investment record.

[151] Pollard, S. (1983) *The Development of the British Economy 1914–1980*. The latest edition of this immensely informative textbook. Like earlier editions [1962; 1969] it still adopts a basically Keynesian view of the world.*

[152] Posner, M. V. (ed.) (1978) *Demand Management*. An examination from different standpoints of both theory and practice.

[153] Posner, M. V. and Steer, A. (1979) 'Price Competitiveness and Performance of Manufacturing Industry', in Blackaby (ed.) [27]. Emphasises non-price factors in competition.

[154] Postan, M. M. (1967) *An Economic History of Western Europe 1945–1964*. An excellent survey. It is particularly good on institutional factors.*

[155] Prais, S. J. (Cambridge, 1976). *The Evolution of Giant Firms in Britain*. Valuable data and analysis though plays down the role of merger activity.

[156] Prais, S. J. (Cambridge, 1981) *Productivity and Industrial Structure: A Statistical Study of Manufacturing Industry in Britain, Germany and*

the U.S. Brings out Britain's relative failure over the past 20 years. By 1975 productivity differences of between 30 and 170 per cent in major industries. Good on plant size and manning practices.

[157] Pratten, C. F. (Cambridge, 1971) *Economies of Scale in manufacturing Industry.* Demonstrates the potential for economies of scale at plant level but emphasises the critical importance of the efficiency of operation – for which there is no easy prescription.

[158] Pratten, C. F. (Cambridge, 1976a) *A Comparison of the Performance of Swedish and U.K. Companies.* More unpalatable fare for the UK based on thorough empirical work.

[159] Pratten, C. F. (Cambridge, 1976b) *Labour Productivity Differentials within International Companies.* Further, excellent empirical work which attempts to apportion the UK's comparative laggard performance between 'economic' and 'behavioural' factors.

[160] Prest, A. R. and Coppock, D. J. (eds) (1966 continuing) *The U.K. Economy: A Manual of Applied Economics.* An invaluable series essential to anyone engaged in serious study of the period.*

[161] Pryke, R. (Oxford, 1981) *The Nationalized Industries: Policies and Performance since 1968.* Generally gives low marks for achievement and prospects.

[162] Purdy, D. and Zis, G. (Manchester, 1974) 'Trade Unions and Wage Inflation in the U.K.', in D. Laidler and D. Purdy (eds), *Inflation and Labour Markets.* A useful critical analysis of the more important literature generated by the original article by Phillips [146].

[163] Radcliffe Report (1959) *Committee on the Working of the Monetary System* Cmnd. 827. *Minutes of Evidence* (1960). *Principal Memoranda of Evidence, 3 vols* (1960). One of the major post-war economic enquiries which contains much valuable information. It revealed that businessmen's investment decisions were little affected by short-run interest rates. Its main fault was narrowness of approach which failed to take account of Britain's underlying, declining economic position.

[164] Rawls, J. A. (Harvard, 1971) *A Theory of Justice.* A modern classic which has attracted much critical discussion, especially among social scientists.

[165] Ray, G. F. (1976) 'Labour Costs in OECD Countries, 1964–75', *National Institute Economic Review,* 78. Comprehensive data which show low UK labour costs per man hour and obversely high labour costs per unit of output.

[166] Reddaway, W. B. *et al.* (Cambridge, 1967) *The Effects of U.K. Direct Investment Overseas: Interim Report*; (Cambridge, 1968) *Final Report.* The general conclusion is that the initial effect was to promote exports and this was followed by a continuing small

positive contribution to the BOP. It is a minefield of assumptions, however.

[167] Robbins, L. (1947) *The Economic Problem in Peace and War.* Emphasises the limited extent to which wartime methods of economic planning have peacetime value.

[168] Robbins Report (1963) *Higher Education* Cmnd. 2154. The tablets justifying the subsequent expansion of higher education.

[169] Rollings, N. (1985) 'The "Keynesian Revolution" and Economic Policy-making: A Comment', *Economic History Review*, 38. Valuable corrective to the 'revolutionary' view. [See 30, 31]

[170] Rowthorn, R. E. (1975) 'What Remains of Kaldor's Law?', *Economic Journal*, 85. The answer is: not much.

[171] Rybczynski, T. M. (1982) 'Structural Changes in the Financing of British Industry and Their Implications', *National Westminster Bank Review*, May. Emphasises the growing 'monetisation' of finance for industry especially through the system of leasing equipment. Correspondingly, points to the relative decline of primary capital markets.

[172] Sargent, J. R. (1979) 'U.K. Performance in Services', in Blackaby (ed.) [27]. Sets out the broad pattern for a sector which needs much more detailed investigations.

[173] Sayers, R. S. (1956) *Financial Policy, 1939–45.* The standard work.

[174] Scammell, W. M. (1980) *The International Economy since 1945.* A very clear basic text.*

[175] Shonfield, A. (1959) *British Economic Policy Since the War.* An invaluable text which argues the case against sterling.*

[176] Shonfield, A. (Oxford, 1965) *Modern Capitalism: The Changing Balance of Public and Private Power.* Particularly useful for its international comparisons.*

[177] Shonfield, A. (Oxford, 1984) *In Defence of the Mixed Economy.* Published posthumously and, as a consequence, is a little unfinished. But it contains interesting ideas and insights.

[178] Singh, A. (1977) 'U.K. Industry and the World Economy: A Case of Deindustrialisation?', *Cambridge Journal of Economics*, 1. An argument for protection.

[179] Smith, D. C. (1980) 'Trade Union Growth and Industrial Disputes' in Caves and Krause (eds) [47]. Basic information and particularly good on comparative international analysis of strike data.

[180] Stewart, M. (1977) *The Jekyll and Hyde Years: Politics and Economic Policy since 1964.* An account sympathetic to Labour governments. Makes a strong demand for so-called responsible Keynesianism and for continuity of economic policy across the two-party divide.

[181] Stout, D. K. (1976) *International Price Competitiveness, Non-Price*

Factors in Industrial Trade. Explains how traditional analysis of the potential effects from devaluation is over-simplified. Contains a very good summary of evidence on non-price factors. An excellent antidote to so much of the literature on exchange-rate theory and policy.

[182] Stout, D. K. (1979) 'Deindustrialization and Industrial Policy', in Blackaby (ed.) [27]. An internationally comparative analysis of productivity and competitiveness.

[183] Strange, S. (Oxford, 1971) *Sterling and British Policy.* An excellent book which examines the issue from the standpoint of international relations.*

[184] Tew, B. (1982) *The Evolution of the International Monetary System 1945–81.* A very good basic textbook.*

[185] Thirlwall, A. P. (1982 edn) *Balance of Payments Theory and the U.K. Experience.* Clear factual account and survey of the literature. Focuses on import penetration and emphasises structural and non-price factors in performance.*

[186] Tomlinson, J. (1984) 'A "Keynesian Revolution" in Economic Policy-Making', *Economic History Review*, 37. The argument that in terms of employment policy there never has been a Keynesian Revolution [30, 31, 169].

[187] Tomlinson, J. (1985) *British Macroeconomic Policy since 1940.* A survey of the literature and an attempt to state the case for a thorough-going application of demand management.

[188] Van Dormael, A. (1978) *Bretton Woods: Birth of a Monetary System.* Good account of the financial diplomacy behind the event.

[189] Verdoorn, P. J. (1949) 'Fattori che regolano lo sviluppo della produttivita del lavoro', *L'Industria.* The original article which caused much controversy.

[190] Walters, A. (1978) *Economists and the British Economy.* A monetarist's attack on Keynesianism and, indirectly, on his whole profession. Written before he became an economic adviser to Mrs Thatcher.

[191] Wells, J. D. and Imber, J. C. (1977) 'The Home and Export performance of U.K. Manufacturing Industry', *Economic Trends*, 286. A detailed, industry by industry analysis of import penetration and export sales ratios for the period 1968–76.

[192] Wiener, M. J. (Cambridge, 1981) *English Culture and the Decline of the Industrial Spirit, 1850–1950.* An impressionistic and selective approach and, for this reason, the thesis advanced may well be thought to be unconvincing. It suffers also from a lack of economic analysis.

[193] Williams, B. R. (Paris, 1962) *International Report on Factors in Investment Behaviour.* A comparative study which reveals that

differences cannot all be explained by numbers – and that there is no alternative, easy explanation.

[194] Williams, K., Williams, J. and Thomas, D. (1983) *Why are the British Bad at Manufacturing?* Management, market limitations, financial institutions and government–industry relations are identified as the villains.

[195] Wilson Committee (1980) *Committee to Review the Functioning of Financial Institutions. Report and Appendices* Cmnd. 7937. An ambivalent and inconclusive report but it contains much useful information.

[196] Worswick, G. D. N. (1970) 'Fiscal Policy and Stabilization', in Cairncross (ed.) [39]. Clear and to the point.

[197] Worswick, G. D. N. and Ady, P. H. (Oxford, 1952) *The British Economy 1945–50.* Still a very valuable collection despite its vintage.

[198] Worswick, G. D. N. and Ady, P. H. (Oxford, 1962). *The British Economy in the 1950s.* Provides good, basic coverage of the main elements.

[199] Wright, J. F. (Oxford, 1979) *Britain in the Age of Economic Management.* Brief, crystal clear and informative.*

Supplementary bibliography

Aldcroft, D. H. (Manchester, 1992) *Education, Training and Economic Performance 1944–1990*. A useful though justifiably gloomy survey of the issues.

Alford, B. W. E. (1995) *Britain in the World Economy since 1880*. An analysis of Britain's relative economic decline in the international economy.

Ashworth, W. (1991) *The State in Business 1945 to the mid-1980s* An excellent, succinct analysis of the nationalized industries.

Cairncross, A. and Watts, N. (1989) *The Economic Section 1939–61: A Study in Economic Advising*. Provides insight into the role of economists in government.

Chick, M. (ed.) (Aldershot, 1990) *Governments, Industries and Markets: Aspect of Government–Industry Relations in the U.K., Japan, West Germany and the United States since 1945*. A source of comparative material.

Collins, B. and Robbins, K. (1990) *British Culture and Economic Decline*. Contains comparative studies of Germany and the USA and surveys the literature.

Harris, J. (1990) 'Enterprise and Welfare States: A Comparative Perspective', *Transactions of the Royal Historical Society*, 40. Also in Gourvish, T. and O'Day, A. (1991). *Britain Since 1945*, Chapter 3. An important critique of Barnett [17].

Kay, J. (Oxford, 1993) *Foundations of Corporate Success: How Business Statistics Add Value*. An excellent study that combines theoretical insight with a firm historical and empirical grasp.

Maddison, A. (Oxford, 1991) *Dynamic Forces in Capitalist Development*. A major source of comparative statistical data but should be used with extreme care. The author does not stress sufficiently the large degrees of error that infect data of this nature.

Milward, A. S. (with the assistance of Brennan, G. and Romero, F.)

(1992) Particularly good on Britain's relations with western Europe between 1950 and 1960.

Pressnell, L. (1986) *External Economic Policy Since the War*. Volume I *The Postwar Financial Settlement*. The authoritative account of British negotiations at Bretton Woods and of the American loan agreement.

Rostas, L. (Cambridge, 1948) *Comparative Productivity in British and American Industry*. A study sponsored by the Board of Trade that revealed a wide gap in productivity levels between British and US industry.

Rowthorn, R. E. and Wells, J. R. (Cambridge, 1987) *De-industrialization and Foreign Trade*. An outstanding analysis which contains much useful statistical data.

Singleton, J. (Oxford, 1991) *Lancashire on the Scrap-heap. The Cotton Industry 1950–1970*. A valuable case study that brings out the persistence of the problem of the old staple industries.

Tomlinson, J. (Oxford, 1994) *Government and the Enterprise since 1900: The Changing Problem of Efficiency*. A comprehensive survey of micro-economic policy.

Van der Wee, H. (1986) *Prosperity and Upheaval. The World Economy 1945–1980*. Provides a good survey of the literature on international economic development during the period.

Index

agriculture 10, 11, 13, 25, 26, 27, 40–1
aircraft industry 38, 56, 64
amalgamation, 54; *see also* business mergers
Argentina 68
Aristotle 91
armed forces, 10, 11; *see also* defence
artificial fibres 31, 57
Atlantic Alliance 19
Austria 6

balance of payments, 20, 34, 48, 65–80; accuracy, 4; crises 67, 68, 70
banking 11, 13, 43, 44, 48
Bank of England 16, 77, 97
Barlow Report 18
Belgium 6, 8, 26, 29, 68
Bentham, Jeremy 91
Beveridge Report (1942) 15
Bevin, Ernest 19, 66
Board of Trade 20, 21
boot and shoe industry 11, 27
Bretton Woods Agreement 18, 65
Bristol 50
'British disease' 9, 95
British Gas 40
British Rail 40
brokerage 48
Brown, George 84
budgets, 22; *see also* demand management
building and contracting 10, 11, 13, 51
building supplies 11, 27
business: capitalisation, 51; concentration, 51–5; management, 55–9, 88, 95–6, 97; mergers, 52, 54, 61–2; organisation 9, 36, 51–9,

89–90, 97; schools, 56; training 45, 56
Butler, R. A. 81
'Butskellism' 24, 81

cable and wireless 16
Canada 68
capital: account, 12; consumption, 30; efficiency, 29; gains, 30, 53; gross, 7; gross per head, 29; growth, 7; human, 44; issues, 18; leasing, 30, 48; markets, 30, 54; net, 7; productivity, 6; shortage, 12; stock, 43; use, 29; *see also* investment
catering industry 49
Central Economic Planning Staff (CEPS) 20
cheap money 17–18
chemical industry 11, 16, 42, 69–70
City of London 66, 77, 89, 95
civil aviation 16
civil engineering 10, 11
civil occupations 10, 11
civil service 9, 83, 94, 96, 97
clothing industry 10, 11, 27
coal miners 16
coal mining 10, 11, 13, 16, 25, 26, 27, 39, 41
coal shortage 19
collective bargaining 23, 24, 61
commerce 11
commercial services 47
commodity trading 48, 57
Commonwealth 16, 18
communism 18, 66
competitiveness 9, 34–9, 69–70, 76–7
Conservative government, 78, 81, 85; Party 24, 41

New Studies in Economic and Social History

Titles in the series available from Cambridge University Press:

Previously published as

Studies in Economic History

Titles in the series available from the Macmillan Press Limited

12. H. McLeod
    Religion and the working classes in nineteenth-century Britain

13. J.D. Marshall
    The Old Poor Law 1795–1834: second edition

14. R.J. Morris
    Class and class consciousness in the industrial revolution, 1750–1850

15. P.K. O'Brien
    The economic effects of the American civil war

16. P.L. Payne
    British entrepreneurship in the nineteenth century

17. G.C. Peden
    Keynes, the treasury and British economic policy

18. M.E. Rose
    The relief of poverty, 1834–1914

19. J. Thirsk
    England's agricultural regions and agrarian history, 1500–1750

20. J.R. Ward
    Poverty and progress in the Caribbean, 1800–1960

Economic History Society

The Economic History Society, which numbers around 3,000 members, publishes the *Economic History Review* four times a year (free to members) and holds an annual conference.

Enquiries about membership should be addressed to

The Assistant Secretary
Economic History Society
PO Box 70
Kingswood
Bristol
BS15 5TB

Full-time students may join at special rates.